POSITIVE **BUSINESS**

Negotiate
for Success

POSITIVE **BUSINESS**

Negotiate
for **Success**

Effective Strategies for Realizing Your Goals

Juliet Nierenberg and
Irene S. Ross

CHRONICLE BOOKS
SAN FRANCISCO

First published in the United States in 2003 by Chronicle Books LLC.

Copyright © 2003 by Duncan Baird Publishers
Text copyright © 2003 by Juliet Nierenberg and Irene S. Ross
Commissioned artwork copyright © 2003 by Duncan Baird Publishers

Conceived, created, and designed by Duncan Baird Publishers Ltd.
Library of Congress Cataloging-in-Publication Data is available.

ISBN: 0-8118-3617-7

Typeset in Bembo
Printed in Singapore

Managing Editor: Judy Barratt
Editors: Joanne Clay, James Hodgson and Yvonne Worth
Managing Designer: Dan Sturges
Designer: 27.12 Design Ltd.
Commissioned Artwork: Melvyn Evans and Howard Read

Distributed in Canada by
Raincoast Books
9050 Shaughnessy Street
Vancouver, B.C. V6P 6E5

10 9 8 7 6 5 4 3 2 1

Chronicle Books LLC
85 Second Street
San Francisco, CA 94105
www.chroniclebooks.com

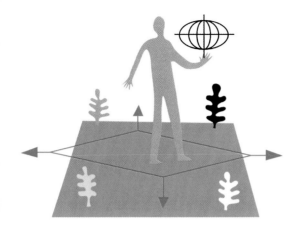

This book is dedicated to Gerard Nierenberg,

Father of Negotiation,

who encouraged us in our work.

CONTENTS

FOREWORD

If there is anything better than having a good friend, it's having a partnership with a good friend. In the 1980s, such a partnership was born.

We met at a 24-hour marathon conference on General Semantics (a discipline devoted to exploring and understanding how we know what we know), in which we are both interested. In our conversations we found that we shared an interest in negotiation as well – Irene, as a lawyer and a judge; Juliet as a former teacher who had started working for the Negotiation Institute, founded by her husband, Gerard, a pioneer in the field of negotiation.

During this era, an increasing number of women were reaching managerial positions and having to call on business negotiation skills. In response to this trend, we created a negotiation seminar especially for women. Our lectures took us to many cities in the United States and Canada, as well as in the Far East and South America. Many of our audiences included men who felt that they, too, were in need of tuning up their negotiation skills!

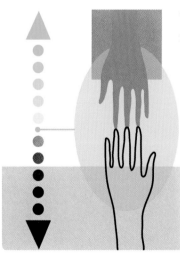

Later we wrote our first book, *Women and the Art of Negotiating*. This was based on our own negotiating experiences. However, it also benefited from the insights we gained from the stories shared with us by participants in our seminars.

Like many people who develop an enthusiasm for a subject, we found ourselves delving ever more deeply into our chosen field. The more we studied negotiation, the less satisfying we found the "do and don't" method provided by most teachings. If every negotiation conformed to a set pattern, a prescriptive list of rules would be perfect. However, every negotiation is unique. When a negotiation develops in an unexpected direction, as is so often the case, the rules no longer apply. Instead, with this book we aim to provide guidelines — a system that makes it possible for a negotiator to prepare for any negotiation, evaluate progress at every step, and assess his or her own contribution to the outcome.

At the heart of our theory of negotiation is the belief that there are essential elements, which we call the Foundation, which apply to all negotiations, whether in a personal or a business context, and that the philosophies of the negotiators determine the direction a negotiation takes. Our experience continues to confirm that an "everybody wins" philosophy, which assures that all parties benefit from a negotiation, creates longer-lasting and more successful outcomes than a "winner takes all" approach. It is not an altruistic philosophy. It is just common sense with a beneficial result. Each of us must take the responsibility for steering a negotiation to a successful conclusion for all.

On a personal note, by applying an "everybody wins" philosophy and the elements of the Foundation, we have found ourselves incredibly enriched and centred in our negotiations, whether they be formal business negotiations, dealings with our friends and family or casual encounters. We hope you will find the same.

Juliet Nierenberg and Irene S. Ross

INTRODUCTION:
A NEW PHILOSOPHY AND A NEW METHOD

Negotiation is the process by which human beings or groups of human beings exchange ideas with each other in order to effect a change in their relationship. Although this book focuses on business-based negotiations, the concepts that it advocates apply to all our dealings.

The most influential factor in the unfolding of a negotiation is the philosophy that informs the conduct of each of the parties involved. Too many people are steeped in the adversarial tradition. They want to win at any cost. However, those who look to gain in the short run by pursuing an "I win, you lose" philosophy risk sacrificing their relationship with the other party in the long run. When the papers are signed and the deal is closed, they may be lulled into believing that all went well, but if the other party remains dissatisfied, believing that they have been disadvantaged or manipulated, it is likely that the wounded party will end the relationship or retaliate in any follow-up dealings.

If we look back on our past negotiations, both in business and in our private lives, we will likely find that we deal with the same people more than once, sometimes on an ongoing basis. If we have been able to achieve results with those people in a mutually supportive spirit, we will generate goodwill that will benefit our future negotiations with them. It is the best guarantee that the negotiated outcome will be implemented and that the results will not come back to haunt us.

It is our basic premise that an "everybody wins" philosophy should underlie every negotiation. By this we mean that the outcome of every negotiation should satisfy all parties involved in it, rather than one party coming away with everything and leaving everyone else unsatisfied.

The key to developing an "everybody wins" philosophy is to consider every aspect of the negotiation from the point of view of the other party or parties as well as our own. What will they want to gain from this negotiation? How will they feel if I make this move or ask that question? Why are they looking anxious – what can I do to reassure them?

Of course, the ideal negotiation requires all parties to share this long-sighted attitude. In reality, this will not always be the case. We cannot expect to be able to change the philosophy of the people with whom we negotiate to match our own. However, we still have to deal with such people. Even when we are faced with someone whose objective is to beat us, we can still steer the negotiation in such a way that both parties get something out of it (see pp.110–11).

Once you have embraced the philosophy, you need a method to put it into practice. For this purpose, we have devised a system that we call the Foundation. By applying the five elements of the Foundation, which we introduce overleaf, to any negotiation, you cannot fail to consider the outcome from the point of view of all parties involved.

pause for reflection (see pp.16–17)

Before any negotiation we take a pause to reflect on the best way to meet our objectives. During the negotiation, we should take a pause whenever we are in danger of saying or doing something that might jeopardize the negotiation or we are uncertain of which direction to take.

search for needs (see pp.18–23)

Two parties negotiate because they each have something that the other needs. In order to reach an outcome that satisfies

THE FOUNDATION

PAUSE FOR REFLECTION

AGREE ON THE FACTS

CONTROL THE CLIMATE

SEARCH FOR NEEDS:
YOUR NEEDS
THEIR NEEDS

MEET YOUR OBJECTIVES

the requirements of both parties, we have to identify not only our own needs but also those of the other party.

determine your objectives (see pp.24–7)

A clear understanding of the needs of both parties enables us to determine objectives that meet our needs but also take account of those of the other party. We may need to pause during the negotiation to revise our objectives, in response to new information or developments.

agree on the facts (see pp.28–33)

In order to reach an agreement with another party, we first need to agree the facts on which we are basing our respective positions. We need to be flexible enough to accept the other party's interpretations when they are justifiable.

control the climate (see pp.34–41)

If we strive to create and maintain a cooperative climate thoughout the negotiation, we show the other party that we are committed to seeking an outcome that satisfies them as well as us. We should consider every move we make in terms of the effect it is likely to have on the negotiating climate.

The diagram, opposite, shows how the elements of the Foundation interrelate. The **pause for reflection** allows you to consider how to discover each party's **needs**, reconcile different interpretations of **facts** and generate a positive **climate** – all of which will help you meet your **objectives**.

chapter 1

PRINCIPLES OF NEGOTIATION

In the introduction to this book we unveiled the five components of the Foundation: pausing for reflection, searching for needs, determining objectives, agreeing on the facts and controlling the climate. In the first part of this chapter we cover these elements in more detail. The Foundation is the lens through which you should watch all of your negotiations unfolding. It enables you to see developments not only from your point of view but also from that of the other party. This "devil's advocate" insight will help you reach a lasting resolution that meets everybody's objectives.

The second section tells you how to assess your strengths and weaknesses as a negotiator and to remould your overall approach to negotiating. For example, you will learn how to be flexible in the face of unexpected changes in the negotiating landscape.

We also look in detail at the practical steps you should take to prepare for a negotiation, such as defining your issues and positions and carrying out objective-focused research.

A FOUNDATION FOR ALL NEGOTIATION:
PAUSE FOR REFLECTION

Before you enter any negotiation, take a long "pause for reflection" to consider what you want from this engagement, what obstacles you may encounter, and how you will overcome them. If you neglect this crucial planning stage, your position will be poorly defined (and, therefore, weak) from the outset and you will be less able to anticipate or react to developments in the negotiation.

A good example of what can happen when there is a failure to pay attention to the elements of successful negotiating was related to us at a seminar. Clara, a sample maker for a designer dress manufacturer, thinking that her job was secure because of her specialist skill, marched into the manager's office at the height of preparations for the

forthcoming season and demanded a substantial raise. She threatened to quit by the end of the week if she didn't receive it. She found the raise in her next pay check, but to her great surprise, she was fired soon after, when the employer found a replacement for her.

Clara would never have engaged in such a gambit if she had taken a pause to reflect on the possible outcomes of such a risky strategy. Having realized that her ultimatum – and, above all, its timing – would threaten the needs (see pp.18–23) of her employer, she would have chosen a less confrontational approach. She might also have spent some time researching the job market (see pp.50–51) to assess how realistic her salary demands were and how easy her employer would find it to replace her.

From time to time during the negotiation, you may pause again – perhaps to cool down if you are close to losing your temper (see pp.94–7), or to review your initial objectives. Clearly, this is easier to do if you are dealing with the other party by fax or e-mail, rather than over the phone or face to face. However, even if you are communicating in "real time", you should still pause to reflect. This may take only a moment. Or, you may feel you have to adjourn proceedings in order to carry out further fact-finding. Don't be afraid to

assert your right to do this, fearing that it will be perceived as a sign of weakness – far better to admit to needing some time than to be swept along while lacking a crucial piece of information to support your position.

SEARCH FOR NEEDS

Needs and their satisfaction are the common denominators in negotiations. Objectives are the results we seek in order to satisfy our needs. For example, if we need to feel more appreciated in our job, we may seek a promotion. If there were no needs to satisfy, there would be no reason to negotiate. Therefore, for successful negotiation, it is necessary to understand what needs are motivating our own objectives and those of the other party. Put simply, if the other party needs something that you can give them and you need something that they can give you, you can negotiate with them.

THE HIERARCHY OF NEEDS

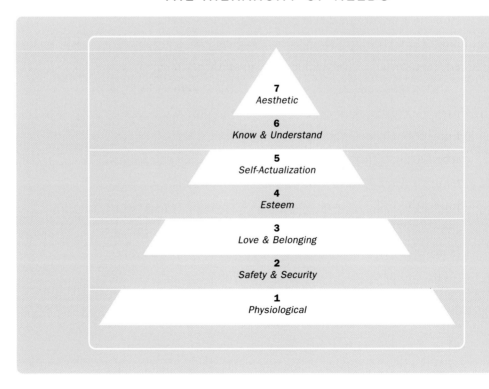

7
Aesthetic

6
Know & Understand

5
Self-Actualization

4
Esteem

3
Love & Belonging

2
Safety & Security

1
Physiological

The psychologist Dr Abraham H. Maslow described seven bundles of needs that influence human behaviour. The pyramid opposite illustrates these needs, with the most fundamental at the base. We have first to satisfy the more basic needs before we become aware of those higher up the pyramid – if you are starving (physiological need), it won't matter to you what colour your wallpaper is (aesthetic). Maslow's hierarchy provides a useful framework for understanding how needs present themselves in negotiations.

physiological needs

Physiological, or homeostatic, needs revolve around the satisfaction of biological drives and urges such as hunger, thirst, fatigue and sex – all of which are manifestations of the body's efforts to maintain itself in a normal, balanced state.

A skilled negotiator, attuned to the needs of all the parties, will prepare a comfortable environment, allowing time for coffee breaks, providing bathroom facilities and scheduling regular mealtime respites during protracted negotiations. An insensitive or aggressive negotiator may urge round-the-clock negotiations until those with less stamina give in. If you find yourself in such a situation, do not accept deprivation. Insist that your physiological needs receive proper attention.

safety and security needs

Most commercial negotiations do not revolve around physiological needs, but they often concern safety and security needs, such as our personal safety, job security and financial well-being. These needs apply not just to individuals but also to business organizations and even countries.

Safety and security needs are a powerful source of motivation, so you should always look for ways in which you can satisfy those of the other party when negotiating with them. For example, imagine that you are a salesperson for a firm that provides anti-virus software. In trying to sell your product to an IT systems manager, you first need to demonstrate to him or her how the software would protect their business interests. Taking care not to be alarmist, you might use evidence to show how common computer viruses are, the harm they can do to a company network and the cost of repairing the damage. Having sold the idea of anti-virus software in general, you are now in a position to sell your company's product in particular.

Sometimes we prioritize the wrong needs, perhaps putting pride above pragmatism, and behave in a way that puts our welfare at risk. Take, for example, the V.P. who quits a lucrative job, because he or she is asked to provide greater accountability and is deprived of the right to choose a secretary. In this case, they would seem to have allowed their esteem needs to override their safety and security needs. To avoid this kind of misjudgment, take a pause for reflection. Always put the most basic need first.

love and belonging needs

While the need to be loved and to belong features particularly prominently in our intimate negotiations, it is important in our working lives as well. An employee who identifies strongly with the company he or she works for will be far more motivated, productive and likely to stay than one who feels alienated in the workplace. In a negotiation, do what you can to make all the people involved feel integral to the process. If there are more than two parties, resist any moves to hold talks with one of the parties that exclude the other party or parties. In face-to-face negotiations, make sure that the seating arrangement does not distance anyone from the heart of discussions, making it harder for them to contribute.

esteem needs

Closely linked with love and belonging needs, esteem needs concern what we think of ourselves and our perception of what others think of us. These needs are commonly expressed in the striving for reputation, status or authority. Often it is a need for esteem as much as a need for money that motivates an employee to negotiate a raise with his or her manager (see pp.134–5). If you are the manager in this situation and your budget does not cover the level of pay increase that your staff member is requesting, seek alternative ways of satisfying their esteem needs until funds are available – for example, by offering them a more prestigious job title.

In any negotiation, respect the esteem needs of the other people involved. Give their contributions due consideration, even if you don't agree with them. Damaging someone's self-esteem can only do harm to the negotiating climate.

self-actualization needs

It is important to feel that you are developing toward your full potential in all walks of your life, including your career. When this need is left unsatisfied – for example, if you are in an unchallenging job with no apparent prospects – it can lead to boredom, frustration and demotivation. If you are negotiating with a previously enthusiastic member of your team over their recent listless performance (see pp.140–41), explore whether their role is fulfilling enough for them. If it is not, find ways of developing their responsibilities into more challenging areas, so that the employee gets the best out of the job and you get the best out of the employee.

the need to know and to understand

It is difficult to negotiate without understanding how the negotiation fits into your company's overall strategy. When preparing, ask yourself not just what you are hoping to achieve from a negotiation, but also why. Discuss these wider issues with your manager, if necessary. Negotiators who have recently joined a new company may be especially in need of this kind of guidance. Being able to see the "bigger picture" will help you to cope if the negotiation develops in a direction that you hadn't planned for. Rather than floundering without your script, you will be able confidently to assess any alternatives that the other party may suggest.

aesthetic needs

It may sound frivolous, but satisfying a need for beauty can contribute to a positive outcome to a negotiation – if you are the host, providing an attractive setting can improve the climate. The other party may be flattered that you value them enough to try to satisfy their aesthetic needs.

WORK SOLUTION 1

Conduct a needs audit

The following exercise provides a system for assessing your needs and those of the other party as you prepare for a negotiation. By considering the key needs on both sides and the objectives that will satisfy these needs, you will be able to approach a negotiation with a focused idea of the main issues to be addressed.

1. In the approach to a negotiation, write out Maslow's hierarchy of seven needs as a list, with physiological needs at the top and aesthetic needs at the bottom. Draw three fairly wide columns next to the list.

2. For each category, give a mark out of 10 for how much potential there is for the upcoming negotiation to satisfy that need, with 0 denoting "no potential" and 10 "enormous potential". Enter the scores into the first column.

3. Pick out any of the needs with high scores (say, 5 and above). Again in the first column, write down objectives that would help you realize the potential to satisfy each of these needs.

4. Now, considering the other party's needs in relation to the negotiation, repeat steps 2 and 3. Force yourself to detach your mind and emotions so that you truly associate yourself with the other party. Write down the marks out of 10, and the objectives that you think the other party should seek, in the second column.

5. Compare the two columns. Look for objectives that coincide and those that conflict. Use the third column to record your conclusions. Commit your needs and objectives audit to memory or take it with you into your negotiation.

DETERMINE OBJECTIVES

It is vital to have a clear understanding of what you want to get out of any negotiation before you get into it. This may seem an obvious point, but all too many negotiators fail to determine their objectives in advance, or lose sight of them during the negotiation, and as a result end up with an unexpected and unacceptable outcome. Your objectives form the cornerstone of your negotiating strategy – all the other elements of the Foundation are geared toward defining and meeting them.

The goals you set for your negotiation should be derived first and foremost from a thorough analysis, based on accurate information, of your needs and those of the other party (see pp.18–23). Ask yourself which issues (see pp.52–3) are most important to you and, to the best of your knowledge, to the other party: price, length of contract, quality, schedule? With this in mind, what would be the optimum deal that you could *realistically* hope for? Are there issues that are relatively unimportant to you but crucial to the other party that you could bargain with to get the best possible outcome on the issues that really do matter to you? How may the objectives of the other party conflict with your own? How will you react if your expectations are not met?

Determining your objectives in advance does not mean that they should be set in stone, come what may. Indeed, your preparations should make you confident enough in the nuances of your position to be able quickly to reassess your targets during the negotiation itself. For example, if the negotiating climate deteriorates, you may decide to offer a concession to restore goodwill. In order to modify your objectives in this way you need to calculate in advance not only what your optimum deal would be, but also what is the "least good" deal that you could accept. Keep this lower threshold in mind throughout the negotiation so that you do not concede ground that you cannot afford to give up. Alternatively, you may (occasionally) discover that discussions proceed more smoothly than you had anticipated. If this happens, ask yourself whether you should revise your objectives upward.

These are the kind of rational thought processes that we should follow to determine our objectives. However, sometimes we allow ourselves to be influenced by negative emotions or compulsions, such as greed, anger or a desire for revenge – perhaps over someone we feel has got the better of us in a previous negotiation. Succumbing to such a negative influence is liable to cloud our judgment. We may find ourselves making difficult or impossible demands that run the risk of antagonizing the other party to such an extent that the dialogue breaks down completely.

Even if we do manage to meet our short-term objective, if the other party feels that we have exploited an unfair advantage that we hold over them, we may jeopardize our long-term relationship with them. Clara the sample maker (see pp.16–17) failed to consider the consequences of making her demand at a time when her presence was essential to manufacturing the next season's line. If she had asked herself the right questions, the stronger, long-term objective of keeping her job would have led her to think twice before issuing her ultimatum. "If I pursue this path, it will likely lead to loss of faith in my good will and loyalty. Even if I get my immediate raise, is it worth the conflict that may result later? Is there another, less confrontational way of getting more pay?" Such an inner dialogue would have pointed to alternative plans. Then she would have had a genuine basis for reaching a decision on how to proceed.

The bottom line is to gain a conclusion that everyone can live with, but we often forget to focus on that goal. Instead, we sometimes act in ways that rebound on us.

After the negotiation is over, take time to debrief yourself. You might find it useful to keep a negotiation journal (see also pp.43–5) in which to record your answers to the following questions. Consider how successful you have been in fulfilling your objectives. If you are satisfied with the outcome, what factors contributed to your success? If the negotiation has not been successful from your point of view, what do you think went wrong? And did you leave the door open for further negotiations? What aspects of your approach would you change? Consider also the success or failure of the negotiation from the other party's point of view? Will they be looking for a way out of the deal because you drove too hard a bargain? Will they look to do business with someone else in the future? By analyzing and learning from each of your negotiations, you will build up a body of experience that will help you establish objectives in future negotiations.

WORK SOLUTION 2

Reflect on what you want

In simple terms, objectives are the results you seek in a negotiation. You can identify them, prioritize them, add to them and change them as the negotiation progresses. You can also make the mistake of not paying enough attention to them in the preparation stage, during the negotiation and even in the aftermath, as you analyze the results. This exercise provides a framework to help you establish your objectives and anticipate those of the other party.

1. Make a wish list of all the objectives you want to achieve in your negotiation – from the mundane to the idealistic. Stretching your imagination in this way may enable you to identify unusual and possibly beneficial approaches that would not otherwise have occurred to you.

2. Decide whether you are seeking short- or long-term goals and consider how the items on your wish list reflect this priority. Rank your objectives in terms of their importance to you.

3. Time for a reality check. Edit the list to eliminate goals that you feel cannot possibly be achieved. However, try to carry into your negotiation the creative frame of mind that enabled you to formulate these ideas.

4. Repeat steps one to three, but this time from the point of view of the other party. By gaining insights into their probable objectives, you may be able to identify which of your objectives are likely to conflict with theirs and prepare ways of resolving these differences at the negotiation phase.

5. Keep these deliberations in mind throughout the negotiation itself, being sure to examine everything that happens in terms of how it affects your objectives.

AGREE ON THE FACTS

Trying to reconcile strongly contrasting and strongly held points of view is often the greatest source of conflict in our negotiations. However, if you are able to meet this challenge, then you go a long way toward clearing the path to a successful outcome for both parties.

We each have our own way of viewing the world, based on the unique set of factors, such as family background, education and cultural influences, that have shaped our personal history. Similarly, two parties in a negotiation, each with their own needs, objectives, biases and philosophies, will inevitably interpret any given issue differently – usually to support their case. For example, in a dispute over pay, labour relations negotiators would probably see all the figures revealed by the

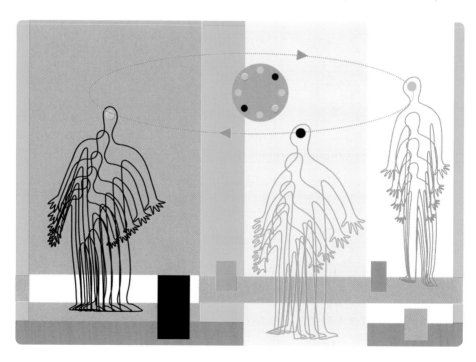

employer as supporting their contention that their members are entitled to a raise, whereas the employer might look at its budget and conclude that it cannot afford both a salary increase and urgent repairs to its factory. George Doris, who served as a principal consultant with a major London-based firm of management consultants, encapsulated the problem in the phrase, "Where you stand depends on where you sit."

Much conflict and confusion in negotiation stems from the common tendency for one or both parties to present their assumptions as facts (see Work Solution 3, p.33). A fact is something that is known to have occurred, to exist or to be true, whereas an assumption is something taken to be true without proof. Sometimes an interpretation can be so deeply ingrained in our thinking that we fail to see that there is no hard evidence to back it up. And sometimes, unfortunately, an unscrupulous negotiator may deliberately disguise assumptions as facts. It is important, therefore, to approach a negotiation in a questioning spirit – to identify assumptions and assess their legitimacy.

Adopt this questioning attitude even before the negotiation. Prepare by examining all the arguments that you plan to use to support your position. Ask yourself whether they are based on verifiable facts or on assumptions. If they are based on facts, make sure that you can produce this evidence if called upon to do so. If your arguments rest on assumptions, such as a forecast of a certain sales level or a judgment about how a key person will act in a particular set of circumstances, consider whether your hypotheses are reasonable. Expect the other party to seize upon your assumptions – be prepared to justify them.

Just as you should consider your position through the eyes of the other party, so you should try to anticipate their arguments. Look for potential weaknesses in their position – assumptions that you would like them to clarify.

The airing and questioning of each party's assumptions can be the most crucial step in resolving an issue. For example, an employee who is passed over for promotion assumes that his or her boss has little faith in their abilities, which causes the employee to lose confidence and retreat within themselves. However, the boss interprets the employee's

THE POWER OF EMPATHY

When we refer to the "other party" in a negotiation, we often think at a purely corporate level. However, negotiators are people, not mere personifications of the companies they represent. Crucial though it is to be able to anticipate the needs, objectives and arguments of the other company involved in a negotiation, it is equally important to be able to appreciate your opposite number's situation on a personal level and to show them that you empathize.

Bear in mind that the person with whom you are negotiating will probably have to "sell" any agreement that he or she reaches to his or her boss, board of directors or company shareholders. You should take the trouble to find out about the difficulties they may face in making this sale. Encourage them to go into as much detail as possible by asking pertinent questions, showing your interest with receptive gestures and facial expressions, and by relating similar problems that you encounter within your company.

This open exchange of experiences will allow you to do two things. Firstly, you will build up a rapport that will make you and the other party feel like partners in the negotiation rather than opponents. This cooperative, empathetic climate (see pp.34–41) will stand you in good stead if you hit a difficult phase in the negotiation. Secondly, you will gain an insight into the workings of the company with which you are dealing that will enable you to present your case in a way that will convince not only the person across the table but also his or her superiors.

introversion as a reluctance to take on additional responsibilities, and concludes that he or she lacks the necessary ambition to progress. This misunderstanding leads to a vicious circle of underperformance and mutual disappointment – until the two parties communicate. When they each become aware of the other's assumptions they can see immediately that they were each mistaken. The boss ensures that the employee is given opportunities to show their abilities and the employee, with confidence renewed, becomes better able to perform. Both the employee and the company benefit.

However, more often than not there is a real difference to resolve between parties entering a negotiation, rather than just a misunderstanding. In order to negotiate with someone who holds an entirely different view of the facts, we must create a climate that enables us to keep communications open until we can bridge the gap. One way of doing this is to start discussions by establishing those areas on which both parties agree, with a view to building up mutual trust and understanding, before moving on to the contentious issues.

The most fruitful way to arrive at an appreciation of how someone else came to their facts is to look methodically at every step they have taken in their calculations or deliberations. You're not trying to demolish their argument, but to identify the stage in their thought process at which their interpretation begins to diverge from yours. Do not gloss over points that seem self-evident to you – it may be that the other party has reached a different, equally valid, conclusion that affects their final position. To give a simple example, if

you are negotiating a delivery date with a supplier, finding out that their plant is about to enter its annual shutdown period will help you to understand why they are unable to commit to your desired schedule. Keep an open mind. If the other party's facts support the negotiation, don't try to hold on to your own at all costs.

One of the biggest fears expressed by unskilled negotiators is that they will be exploited, suffer loss of esteem, or lose the deal if they are shown to lack a key piece of information. Well, it's a pretty safe assumption that the other side will know something that you don't, because it is not possible to know everything. The information that each party brings to the negotiation, and shares with the other party, is crucial in reaching a successful outcome. Agreement on the facts is more important than whose facts they are.

Where both parties remain wedded to opposing interpretations but desire that negotiations continue, they can agree to be bound by the findings of fact of a mutually agreed third party. This is often a primary responsibility of arbitrators (see p.146).

We should expect that the other people in our negotiations will present facts that conflict with our own and which validate their own points of view. Successful negotiators can, however, through mutual effort made possible in a positive climate, resolve initial differences in interpretation of facts and arrive at a consensus. A fact, by this definition, becomes a fact because both parties have agreed upon it. One more step toward creating a successful negotiation.

WORK SOLUTION 3

Recognize the assumptions

A common ploy among people with a forceful personality, a dogmatic debating style or a weak negotiating position is to present their assumptions and opinions as incontestable fact. Such statements often raise the temperature of the encounter, turning a negotiation into an argument. The following exercise in communication analysis is designed to help you recognize this technique – both in yourself and in other people – and to find ways of counteracting it.

1. Find some source material for your analysis. This could be a political debate on TV or radio, a business meeting, or even one of your everyday conversations – anything that involves the airing of more than one point of view.

2. In your source material, listen for contentious statements that are based on assumption but presented as fact and take a note of them, either literally or mentally. Examples of this type of assertion include: "Big cars are definitely safer" or "She leaves us in no doubt that she's not a team player."

3. Taking each of the statements in turn, assess the validity of the assumption on which it is based. What techniques does the speaker use to reinforce his or her point? Think about all aspects of the speaker's delivery – not just phraseology but also intonation and body language. What effect do the statements have on you – do they anger you, intimidate you, baffle you?

4. How would you amend these statements in terms of their expression and their delivery to make it clear that they are based on assumptions rather than fact (for example, "She doesn't seem like a team player to me")? How might these modifications affect the climate of a negotiation? Practise this technique whenever you can, and use it to clarify your position in future negotiations.

CONTROL THE CLIMATE

Every negotiation has its own climate – a prevailing mood that influences the way in which the negotiation develops and is itself governed by the way in which the participants behave. You can discern how people are relating to each other by observing clues such as the tone of their voice, the words they use, their gestures and where they place themselves in the negotiating room. It is important to negotiate in a positive climate – one in which both parties are keen to work together to find a mutually satisfactory solution – if you are to achieve your objectives. Fortunately, unlike the weather, there are ways in which you can exert some measure of control over the climate in a negotiation.

The guiding principle behind your efforts to control the climate must be to show the other party that you have their interests at heart as well as your own. If you are able to foster a cooperative climate in this way, the other party is more likely to approach disagreements with a view to solving them rather than escalating them. They will see every issue that is resolved as a step toward the overall outcome, making them even more committed to finding solutions for the issues that remain. They will be more inclined to make concessions if they see that you want both parties to benefit.

The early stages of a negotiation are particularly important in the climate-building process, as this is when the tone is set. Even before the negotiation you have the chance to

demonstrate that you are aware of the other party's needs – by calling the meeting at a time that is convenient for them rather than coercing them into fitting in with your schedule. If you are the host, be hospitable. Make the visiting negotiators feel at ease and welcome. Make sure of adequate and comfortable seating in a room that is set at a comfortable temperature. Position the parties in a non-confrontational seating arrangement, rather than ranging them along opposite sides of a meeting-room table. If the negotiation is being held in your office, don't stay behind your desk. This aggressive statement of authority and superiority will most likely make the other party feel intimidated and on their guard – not a good basis on which to build a positive climate. Focus your full attention on the negotiation, rather than giving the impression that you are rushed or preoccupied with other matters, and make sure that your calls are held. Show your interest in the other party by addressing them by name and take the trouble to find out some of their background if possible. Allow some time for "small talk". All the while, get an impression of their attitude by closely observing their gestures (see pp.72–5). Do they seem critical and somewhat unfriendly? Are they signalling impatience by word or body language? If so, take a cue from them and get on with the formal proceedings.

As the negotiation progresses, you should continue to monitor the climate. Carry on observing the nonverbal behaviour of the other party and treat it as a barometer of changes in their attitude. For example, at the outset of a negotiation you may deduce that your opposite number is in a relaxed state of mind from signs such as open hand gestures, an unbuttoned jacket and receptive facial expressions. As the negotiation proceeds, you see a change in their physical demeanour: they fold their arms across their chest, they cross their legs, they point their index finger at you, and make agitated hand movements. These signs are evidence that their attitude has changed from receptive to defensive, leading to a tougher negotiating climate. Ask yourself what might have brought about this change. Have you done anything to threaten their needs? What can you say or do to reasssure them? If you cannot explain the change in the mood of the other party, consider asking them directly

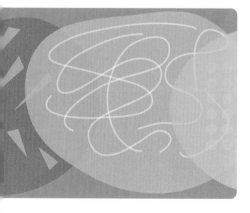

whether something is bothering them and
what you can do to help. However, the direct
approach should be handled with care – if
there is any hint of aggression or exasperation
or condescension in your manner, you may
harden the other party's negative attitude.

We can't control the thoughts, feelings and actions of
other negotiators (it's hard enough to control our own). But
in being responsible for pursuing a positive climate at all
times, we exercise a large degree of influence over the direction in which the negotiation progresses. There are as many
climates as there are negotiations, and you should treat each
on its own merits. However, there are certain types of climate
that will strike a chord with most negotiators. Below are
general guidelines on how to tackle some of the most common of these climates.

the hostile climate

Hostility often results from one party infringing the needs of
the other. Perhaps the other party feels that you have snubbed
them in some way, thereby threatening their need for esteem.
If so, do what you can to repair the damage by ensuring that
you pay them due respect. Or an unscrupulous negotiator
may inject hostility into the climate in order to intimidate
the other party into a deal that threatens their safety and
security needs. If you suspect this is happening to you, build
an airtight case for your position to show your resolve.
Remain friendly but firm.

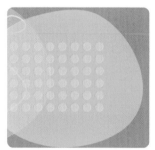

Above all, if you are faced with a hostile climate, stay calm and focused on your objectives. Listen hard to what the other party is saying. Try to identify their grievances and how you can address them. If the other party is angry, let them express themselves without interrupting them. Reiterate your resolve to find a solution that benefits all parties.

the bored climate

Boredom may be signalled by gestures such as doodling, fingers drumming softly on the table, head cradled in hands, a blank stare. If you observe any of this kind of body language in the other party, think of ways to recapture their attention. Have you been negotiating for a long time – should you suggest breaking off for coffee or for lunch? Have you been spending too long on a particular issue – should you introduce a new point?

the suspicious climate

It is difficult to make progress if one side distrusts the other. If you feel that the other party is suspicious of you, you may have failed to convince them that your aim is to reach a fair result. Explain to them how your proposals will benefit them as well as you.

the disorganized climate

Valuable time can be wasted if one or both of the parties have not prepared adequately. In particular,

WORK SOLUTION 4

Keep the climate positive

Nurturing a positive climate is a key negotiation tool. And who is responsible for keeping the climate positive? You are! You cannot predict or control another person's behaviour. However, you can control how you respond. If you sense that the mood of your negotiation is deteriorating, ask yourself the following questions to help you analyze and respond to the negative climate.

1. First, try to understand the behaviour of the other party. What emotion are they expressing? Look for clues in their words, the tone of their voice and their body language. Has their demeanour altered since the beginning of the negotiation or since the last time you met them? If so, in what way?

2. Ask yourself what might have provoked their negative behaviour. For example, might they be responding to pressure from their superiors? Or might they be reacting to something that you have said or done?

3. Having identified the nature of the negative climate and explored possible causes, think of appropriate ways to counteract the climate. What approach will help to neutralize its harmful effects (see box, p.40)?

4. Monitor your own emotions. Can you feel your temper rising? Are you showing your irritation in the form of signs such as exasperated facial expressions, sighing or shaking of your head? Will your schedule allow an adjournment? If so, go for a walk to clear your head, or, to relieve your frustration, address an angry letter or e-mail to the person who is annoying you, but do not send it. When you reconvene, you and the other party should be in a more positive frame of mind and better able to resolve the issues that still divide you.

if the negotiation is proceeding without an agenda, break off discussions in order to agree on one. Once you have drawn up an agenda, ensure that you stick to it.

the overfriendly climate

Inexperienced negotiators may slip into overfriendliness to disguise a lack of confidence. The negotiation may struggle to get beyond the small talk. If this happens, remain business-like, without being unfriendly. Guide discussions toward the agenda and nip digressions in the bud (see pp.100–103).

the tense climate

When a negotiation is close to boiling point, you need to release the pressure. Suggest taking a break or try to inject some humour. However, be careful not to give the impression that you are joking at the expense of the other party.

TWO WRONGS DON'T MAKE A RIGHT

A prevailing mood can be infectious – if you come up against hostility, it's hard to stop yourself from reacting in a hostile way. However, every negative climate has an antidote. If you find the right response, you can neutralize the effects of any damaging atmosphere. The table below gives some examples of positive responses to negative climates.

NEGATIVE CLIMATE	POSITIVE RESPONSE
Agitated	Calming
Apathetic	Dynamic
Defensive	Supportive
Dogmatic	Creative
Hostile	Helpful
Prejudiced	Open-minded
Suspicious	Open
Thoughtless	Considerate
Unprincipled	Ethical

WORK SOLUTION 5

Make a negotiation mantra

It's not always possible to break off from a negotiation to cool down when you feel anger, frustration, fear or some other strong emotion welling up inside you. At such times, the use of a mantra or affirmation – a repeated word, phrase or statement designed to instil a particular message in you – can restore your calm and remind you of your objectives and the best way to achieve them. At the simplest level, repeating "Objectives–Needs–Climates" to yourself is a quick, easy way to keep the Foundation at the front of your mind, but you can also devise affirmations that relate to specific negotiating situations.

1. If you have the opportunity, spend some time preparing affirmations at the same time that you are preparing for the negotiation as a whole. Try to anticipate the potential threats to the climate of this particular negotiation and tailor your affirmations accordingly. For example, if you are an entrepreneur with a small business negotiating with a large corporation and you are worried that you may be steamrollered, think of a statement to help you stand up for yourself – perhaps "I have something that they need."

2. Think also of affirmations to counteract weaknesses in your negotiating skills (see pp.42–5). For example, if you are quick to anger, you might use a statement such as "I will control my temper, I will control the climate, I will achieve my goal."

3. During the negotiation, if negative messages (for example, "Uh-oh, I'm in trouble now" or "I can't deal with this idiot") jam your internal airwaves, chase them away by repeating soundlessly to yourself one of your prepared affirmations. If none of them is appropriate or if you haven't had a chance to prepare any, just make one up on the spot. Identify the negative emotion you are feeling and create a mantra to counter it. For example, if you are starting to panic: "Stay calm – you can do it."

BUILDING ON THE FOUNDATION:
DEVELOPING A NEGOTIATING STYLE

We have seen how important it is to understand the behaviour and motivations of the people with whom we negotiate. However, we also need to appreciate our own negotiating characteristics if we are to get the most out of our transactions. If we know where our strengths lie, then we can find ways of playing to them. Similarly, an awareness of those of our traits that are detrimental to the negotiating process is the necessary first step toward correcting them.

The task of assessing our negotiating style is complicated by the fact that it is often deeply ingrained in us from childhood. It can be difficult for us to pick out traits in ourselves that we display without thinking. The following steps are designed as a framework to help you to identify your negotiating strengths and weaknesses, set yourself appropriate personal performance objectives, and monitor your progress in meeting them. All you need is your negotiation journal (see p.26), a few minutes now and before and after each of your negotiations, and the desire to maximize your effectiveness as a negotiator.

stage 1: identify your negotiating style

Read the following list of statements and for each one decide whether you: agree strongly; agree somewhat; neither agree nor disagree; disagree somewhat; or disagree strongly.

- *I lose my temper easily.*
- *I prefer to back down rather than risk a confrontation.*
- *If I don't get everything I want, I feel that I have failed.*
- *I find it difficult to make decisions.*
- *I rush into decisions that I later regret.*
- *Ironing out the details bores me.*
- *I'm good at suggesting new ways of looking at a problem.*
- *I hate arriving at a meeting feeling unprepared.*
- *I enjoy being centre stage.*
- *People often don't seem to understand what I'm trying to say.*

If possible, also ask one or two of your colleagues – preferably people who have attended negotiations with you – to consider which of the statements apply to you. This will help you to gain an objective picture.

Gather together the sets of results and in your journal write down a list of conclusions that present themselves. Try to divide them into two groups: negotiating strengths and weaknesses. This isn't a cut and dried process – some attributes can be either a strength or a weakness depending on the circumstance. For example, preferring to back down to avoid a confrontation may be an asset – a way of showing flexibility for the long-term good of the negotiation. Conversely, it may be construed as a failing if it means that you are easily intimidated and manipulated by more overbearing negotiators.

stage 2: set your performance goals

It is now time to devise a strategy based on the findings you made at stage one. Looking first at the list of your strengths, write down in your journal specific ways in which you can use these qualities in your negotiations. For example, if you and your colleagues agree that you are good at tackling problems in unusual ways, set yourself the task of creating imaginative alternatives (see pp.46–8) in order to avoid deadlocks. If you are diligent in your preparations, assume responsibility for drawing up the agenda. If you enjoy being centre stage, use your fondness for the limelight to steer the negotiation or to act as a spokesperson for your team. However, ensure that you do not dominate the meeting: challenge yourself to be aware of the nonverbal behaviour (see pp.72–5) of other people present, which may betray their resentment at your having upstaged them.

Repeat this goal-setting process for the weaknesses that you have pinpointed. Consider what practical steps you can take in your negotiations to bolster the areas that require attention. For example, if you are quick to anger, train yourself to recognize the signs that you are on the way toward losing your temper. Nip your anger in the bud – perhaps by breathing deeply (see p.97) or by repeating a mantra to yourself (see p.41) to keep focused on your objectives.

In some cases you may need to decide whether to counteract a weakness or whether to make a virtue of it. For example, if you tend to shun the centre stage, should you try to play a more prominent part in a negotiation, or should you exploit your position in the wings to observe the way the negotiation is developing and advise your colleagues?

stage 3: track your progress

From now on, when you are preparing for a negotiation, you should consider how to meet not only your business objectives but also the personal development targets that you set yourself at stage two. Write down in your journal what you hope to achieve. Each negotiation is different, so each offers different ways to hone your skills. For example, having to agree on a lengthy and complicated contract in a short space of time might offer the opportunity to work in particular on your time-management skills or your eye for detail.

After the negotiation, go back to your journal and record how successful you feel you have been in meeting your aims. What aspects of your performance were you happy with? Where can you improve next time? Did you learn anything, positive or negative, from the way that any of the other people present tackled the negotiation?

TAKING A FLEXIBLE APPROACH

Like most other areas of our business lives, negotiating is a dynamic, on-going process, not a static system. At every moment, each party has to reconsider its position in the light of actions taken by another party. In our preparations, we try to anticipate a variety of possible outcomes so that we can minimize our own missteps, but we also have to accept that developments other than those for which we have planned will occur. How we respond will have a huge bearing on the outcome of the negotiation.

One approach would be to stick rigidly and unquestioningly to your original plan, even if it is completely incompatible with the other party's requirements. However, if you insist on achieving one hundred per cent of your objectives come what may, you are more likely to end up with one hundred per cent of nothing when the other party walks away. And an inflexible attitude does not only damage your negotiations, it can also affect your sense of well-being –

if you are unable to take surprises in your stride, you are likely to become tense and anxious when they arise.

It is at times of uncertainty that the elements of the Foundation come into their own. Not only do you use the Foundation to prepare for your negotiation, but you can also call on it to help you cope when an unforeseen development blows a hole in your preparations.

For example, an issue that you had thought would be easily resolved, or even an issue that you didn't realize existed, may turn out to be an unexpected sticking point. Let's say that you are a printer supplying brochures to accompany a launch presentation. Your client tells you at short notice that the date of the presentation has to move forward by a week, giving you less time in which to deliver. You calculate that even if you run at absolute maximum capacity, you will be able to deliver only half of the order by the revised deadline. If you were unable to see beyond this obstacle, then the deal would be dead. You would miss out on the business and, without brochures, your client's launch would fall flat. This is a time to be creative.

Taking a pause for reflection, you realize that if the deadline cannot change, you need to find out what can. You talk to your client to assess his or her needs. Apart from anything else, this reassures them that you are making an effort to find a solution to their problem, which helps to keep the climate positive. Is their budget fixed? If not, you might suggest subcontracting some of the order to another printer at an additional cost. Perhaps some time could be saved by missing out a "luxury" element of the specifications – say, blocking the company's name in gold leaf on the cover? Does your client need all of the brochures for the launch itself, or can some of the order be delivered later to be used in follow-up mailouts?

Being *prepared* to be flexible does not mean that you always have to *be* flexible. Take the following situation. You are negotiating the sale of a product to another company. Discussions are proceeding smoothly and the terms of the contract have almost been finalized when the other party suddenly threatens to pull out unless you drop your price. If the deal is worth rescuing, you should stop to ask yourself some questions. Has there been a real change in the other party's circumstances – perhaps a downturn in profits or a change of ownership – that might explain their revised position, or do you suspect that it is a ploy? If their situation has changed, consider whether you should revise your price objective in order to reflect their changed needs. However, if you suspect a ruse, you may decide to hold firm.

While recognizing that negotiations do not always evolve in the way we had anticipated, and taking account of unforeseen developments, we should not let them distract us from our objectives. What is required above all is a flexible yet focused approach. A problem may not be of your making, but if you display the imagination, the persistence and the generosity to find a solution, your efforts will be rewarded with a successful outcome to your negotiation and the goodwill of the other party – a solid basis for a productive and long-lasting business relationship.

WORK SOLUTION 6

Stretch your body to stretch your mind

Physical stretching does not only benefit the body. Studies have shown that people whose joints and muscles are supple and relaxed are more likely to demonstrate the mental flexibility that is so important for negotiation. In order to maximize your physical flexibility, consider enrolling in supervised classes in a stretching discipline, such as yoga. In the meantime, the exercise below is a simple routine to get you started – it's particularly good for those who spend a large proportion of their working day hunched at a desk reading or typing.

1. Standing behind a chair with your knees slightly bent, stretch your arms over your head and bend gently forward at the hips until your upper body is at 90° to your legs. Take hold of the back of the chair and extend your neck and spine and your fingers as far as you can. Hold this stretch for around 10 seconds.

2. Next, sit on the chair and face directly forward with your head perfectly aligned with your neck and spine. Breathing out, turn your head as far to the right as you can without forcing it. Breathing in, return to the centre. Then turn your head to the left in the same way. Repeat this neck stretching for about 2 minutes.

3. Still sitting on the chair, and keeping your upper body straight, gently twist from your hips so that your chest comes to face the back of the chair. Hold on to the back of the chair with both hands and look over your shoulder in the direction of the twist. Although the aim is for your chest to face the back of the chair, only twist as far as is comfortable. Repeat the twist in the opposite direction.

4. Perform this routine regularly. Although it might raise eyebrows if you were to try it in the middle of a face-to-face negotiation, look for a quiet spot to practise it during a break – especially if you are searching for a solution to a deadlock.

DOING YOUR RESEARCH

Although the elements of the Foundation are universally applicable, each negotiation scenario has its particular set of information that you need to have at your fingertips in order to define and meet your objectives. In your preparations you will invariably need to use a variety of research techniques to gather this information.

Most crucial of all is information that relates directly to the issues at the heart of your negotiation. Suppose your objective is to negotiate a large annual bonus. If your research into your company's results indicates a serious downturn, you will probably have to set a more achievable objective, perhaps increased vacation time or more flexible working hours.

You may be lucky and hit upon a published source in print or on the Internet that tells you everything you need to know. However, it is more likely that you will have to conduct your own fieldwork. This may entail shopping around for comparison purposes or – for an important transaction – you may even commission a market research study. For example, a retailer negotiating with a developer over the

siting of an outlet in a shopping mall might invest in their own analysis of pedestrian traffic to verify the developer's data.

If you are dealing with another company, it can be useful to do some research into the way the organization operates. You may gain an insight that influences your strategy. For example, if a company dictates that any settlement its negotiators reach be ratified by two board directors, ensure that you do not trample over this process in your haste to get them to sign.

Try also to find out about the individuals with whom you will be negotiating. Talk to colleagues who have dealt with them before. Understanding what makes a person tick will help you to adapt your negotiating style to match his or hers for the good of the climate. For example, if a colleague tells you that the person with whom you will be negotiating can be impatient and ill-tempered when discussions get bogged down, do what you can to keep the negotiation moving – perhaps suggest coming back to the details later.

Let's look at a case study. You are reviewing a continuous contract for circuit boards with a supplier in southeast Asia. The supplier is demanding a ten per cent price increase, claiming a rise in the cost of raw materials and shipping, and you want to check the validity of their position. You decide to subscribe to a raw materials price index and you get in touch with a friend who works in shipping whom you first met on an airplane (networking is another valuable research skill!). You also get prices from your supplier's main competitors. Your research tells you that the cost of raw materials and shipping has remained steady and that your supplier's desired price increase would make them five per cent more expensive than their nearest rival. What's more, your chief financial officer points out that your suppliers are approaching the end of their financial year, which makes you suspect that they will be keen to agree a deal. Armed with this information, you are able to push for a price that will suit both parties.

DEFINING ISSUES AND POSITIONS

In preparing for a negotiation, it is vital to assess and prioritize your own issues and positions, and to make an educated
guess, based on research, as to what those of the other party
are likely to be. Issues are the specific areas of disagreement
to be discussed during a negotiation, while positions are the
outcome each side says they want. Your opening position
represents what you hope to achieve from the negotiation in
a best-case scenario. Your objective is less ambitious, but
would still represent a satisfactory outcome for you. The
absolute minimum point below which you cannot go is your
need. The aim of the negotiation will be to satisfy the needs,
and ideally the objectives, of each party.

Begin by defining your main need and objective. For
example, if you are negotiating the sale of 500 desk lamps, and
you calculate your lowest acceptable unit price to be $42,
then that sum represents your need. If you would be happy to
accept $46, that price is your objective. However, you choose
the price of $50 as your opening position because it will
allow you to compromise during the negotiation if necessary
and still come away satisfied. Avoid setting your opening position too high, as this can antagonize the other party.

Next identify the issues to be tackled. In the above scenario, the buyer's opening position might be that he or she
will only pay $40 per lamp. The disputed $10 is your central
issue. There may also be other issues to be negotiated, such as
the payment and delivery methods. It is helpful to list all your
issues, as well as those the other party might raise, in order of
priority. Think about the order in which you plan to present

your issues. For example, you may decide to put a minor issue on the table first, so as to create a good climate right at the beginning by conceding on that particular point.

Set your position, objective and need on each issue before the negotiation begins. If during the discussion the two parties appear to reach a stalemate, then you need to modify your opening position. Making concessions in this way allows you to restore a climate of trust and credibility, and increases both parties' chances of reaching a satisfactory outcome. Entering the negotiation with clearly defined positions and objectives gives you the flexibility and confidence to compromise without feeling that you have "lost" something.

Bear in mind that there can be drawbacks to position-based negotiating. If one or both of you has an over-inflated opening position, there is a risk that you will waste time "haggling" and trying to guess what the other party's real objective is, endangering the climate. In that situation, try to explain gently to the other party that their entrenched position threatens the whole process. Remember that positions are just a starting point – the task in a negotiation is to deal with the important issues, refrain from getting stuck in positions, and to seek a resolution that will satisfy both parties.

CHOOSING YOUR TACTICS

Tactics are the individual moves you make during a negotiation to implement your plan or strategy. Let's say you're seeking a raise in salary. Your overall strategy may be to convince your boss how important you are to the business. Your tactics might include using graphs or other data to show how your department has progressed under your leadership, enlisting another department head to sing your praises, or outlining a game plan for the next improvement you intend to implement.

The term "tactic" has connotations of games-playing, points-scoring and one-upmanship that are at odds with the "everybody wins" philosophy that underpins all lastingly successful negotiations. Tricking your way to your objective

at the expense of the relationship is a hollow achievement. For example, if you use anger as a tactic to force the other side to make a concession, you may be surprised by their stiff resistance to being manipulated in this way and end up playing out the rest of the negotiation with a wary opposer. Any negotiations with the same party will be more difficult next time, if not precluded altogether. Similarly, a real estate broker whose fee is withheld by a landlord until the broker has to threaten the landlord with a lawsuit will not steer a client to that landlord's property a second time. In a broker-driven business, this withholding tactic is a foolish policy on the part of the landlord.

However, there are times in a negotiation when a well-judged ploy can accelerate the progress of both parties toward a mutually satisfactory outcome. Even tactics that seem blatantly manipulative can be justifiable if used with the interests of both parties in mind. Take the following situation. You have been drawing up a contract. Negotiations have been protracted owing to the excessively pedantic approach of a member of the other team. If the contract is not finalized in the three days that remain before an important trade fair, there is a danger that it will be too late to rescue the deal. At last you are at the contract-signing stage, but you object to a certain, relatively minor, clause. Rather than raising it as an issue and wasting time with a detailed discussion, you decide to strike out the clause, initial it and send the contract to the other party for signing. You hope that the other members of the other team, recognizing your *fait accompli* to be for the good of the deal as a whole, will over-rule the "nit-picker".

Deciding whether it is acceptable to use a tactic requires careful consideration. Work Solution 7 (see p.59) and the appraisals of some of the most common tactics, below, are designed to help you make that call.

forbearance

To forbear is to do nothing when the other party might have expected a reaction from you. Instead you wait for their next move. It can be an effective response when you feel that the other party is trying to intimidate or provoke you with a

manufactured outburst or a barbed comment. Forbearance is a non-confrontational method to let them know that you won't be swayed. The pause that you introduce into the proceedings in this way gives the other party the chance to reflect that they are wasting their time and would be better advised taking a more constructive approach. However, ask yourself whether you have done anything to justify their hostility. If so, ignoring them will only worsen the climate.

good guy/bad guy

This tactic is so well known that it is almost a cliché, yet it is used frequently despite the fact that it is so recognizable. One partner assumes the role of tough, unrelenting antagonist. The other partner, the good guy, will resurrect the deal by softening the harsh stand his or her partner has taken. The intention is to make the other party feel indebted to the good guy for saving the negotiation, and therefore more willing to make concessions. This highly manipulative tactic may occasionally be appropriate – perhaps as a last-ditch attempt to create movement in an unusually obstinate negotiator.

If you suspect that the other party is acting out a good guy/bad guy routine, the key is to let them know that you recognize the ploy. If you stay calm and friendly, you can be frank without damaging the climate. Indeed, an injection of straight-talking may be what is needed to focus both parties' attention on their responsibility to reach a fair outcome.

salami

This tactic takes its name from the principle that if you want someone to give you their salami, it's better to ask them for a slice at a time than to demand the whole salami at once. Let's say that you are trying to sell a particular component to a large company. Through research you discover that the company is buying its total supply from a single source. You initially offer to supply ten per cent of the total requirement at a knockdown price for a trial period. Through competitive pricing, high quality and reliable delivery, you gradually build up your order until you're the one with the whole salami.

If the salami tactic is used on you, then it is clear that you have something that the other party is keen to acquire – ensure that you get something in return. If they want a cut of your business, let them know that they have to do better than your existing supplier if you are to give them any more.

the hurry-up

If you want to pressurize the other party into concluding a deal quickly and on your terms, you may set them an artificial deadline. For example: "If you don't order now, we can't deliver on time"; or "Prices go up next week. This is the last opportunity to order at the old price." This may be a justifiable way of countering deliberate time-wasting. However, if you overuse this tactic, it will lose its impact and may jeopardize your relationship with the other party.

If the other party tries to hurry you up, ask questions to understand their motives. If you suspect that they are trying to panic you into making a concession, stand your ground. Remind yourself and the other party that you have something that they need. If you are to give it to them, it must be on your terms as well as theirs.

changing levels

As a last resort in a deadlocked negotiation when you feel that the people with whom you're negotiating are being unreasonably intransigent, you might consider trying to deal instead with their superiors. This move is likely to drive a wedge between you and the original team, but on the other hand it may salvage the negotiation and your future relationship with the company as a whole.

If you are on the receiving end of this tactic, swallow your pride. Calmly assess whether the other party has grounds for going over your head. Focus on repairing the damaged climate by being more attentive to their needs.

WORK SOLUTION 7

The line judge

In the heat of a negotiation, it is all too easy to overstep the mark. You may be tempted to engage in foul play to gain an unfair advantage over the other party. But any short-term benefit you may gain will be far outweighed by the damage you will do to your long-term relationship with them. When you are contemplating using a tactic, you should refer your decision to your private line judge – ask yourself the following questions to assess whether what you are planning is in the spirit of an "everybody wins" negotiation.

1. What is your overriding feeling toward the other party at this point in the negotiation? Do you feel respect? Warmth? Exasperation? Contempt? Has your opinion of them changed since the beginning of the negotiation? If so, how?

2. Thinking as objectively as you can about the tactical move that you are contemplating, what are your motives for using it? Do you think that it will get the negotiation moving for the good of both parties? Is the ploy a means to gain revenge? Or is it a way of squeezing the last drop out of the deal?

3. Based on your experience of them, how do you think the other party would react to the tactic? Would they even realize that you were using a tactic? How would you respond if the other party did to you what you are planning to do to them?

4. If you decide to go ahead with the tactic, what will you do if the other party reacts badly to it? For example, will you apologize and withdraw? Or will you persist, explaining how your scheme ultimately benefits them as well as you?

5. There is no magic formula to tell you when it is or isn't acceptable to resort to a tactic. However, your answers to these questions should confirm your instincts.

chapter 2

SKILLS THAT MAKE NEGOTIATIONS WORK

Some people love to negotiate and are comfortable with the process. For others, less confident in their abilities, negotiation can be terrifying.

In this chapter we offer some important skills to add to your toolbox, whatever your current attitude toward negotiation. At the heart of all of these skills is the Foundation. For example, the most pivotal negotiation skill – clear communication – is essential in conveying your needs and objectives to the other party and in understanding theirs. It also allows you to establish where your interpretation of the facts differs from theirs and to find a way of bridging the gap. Above all, the five pillars of effective communication – succinct talking, active listening, constructive questioning, positive body language and avoidance of "meta-talk" – work together to engender a positive, cooperative negotiating climate. A positive climate provides a platform to enable you to display the skills of enlightened persuasion and informed decision-making that take you the rest of the way toward a successful outcome for both parties.

COMMUNICATION

Communication is the engine of business negotiation just as it is the central part of all our other interactions. However, in negotiations communication is not limited to straightforward listening and speaking – it also embraces meta-talk (the hidden meaning behind words) and writing, as well as a range of other highly expressive nonverbal methods of communication. Effective communication is essential for effective negotiations – such discussions succeed or fail as a direct function of the parties' abilities to communicate with each other.

To communicate successfully, you need to follow some basic principles. Be mindful of the elements of the Foundation (see chapter 1), which include careful preparation, thinking about the objectives and needs of all the parties, and keeping the climate positive. Listen attentively to what the other party has to say and ensure what you say is clear and succinct. Avoid technical jargon as much as possible – the more basic the language the more effective it is. Check regularly that both parties are registering the same message by asking questions such as, "Do I understand you to mean such and such?" or "Did I explain that clearly enough?" Throughout the negotiation, meticulously observe the messages the other person is transmitting through their body-language and meta-talk – this will give you important clues about their true thoughts and feelings.

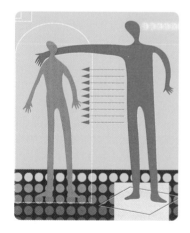

For example, imagine that the firm you represent is bidding to become the new internet-service provider for a large insurance company and you are in negotiation with the company's technical manager. Well-prepared, you are knowledgeable about the company and you listen attentively while the manager explains his needs, occasionally asking leading questions to ensure that you get all the information you require. You then outline the services you are offering and their cost briefly without resorting to complex technical language. When you notice that the manager is showing signs of anxiety – he has his hand over his mouth and won't look you in the eye – you seek to reassure him by asking him to tell you exactly what he is unhappy about. His worries about cost are then successfully ironed out in further discussion and the deal that is reached is satisfactory to you both.

Now imagine that you arrive at the same meeting knowing nothing about the company. This may well irritate the manager, who, as a result, does not take care to explain his needs clearly. Lacking essential information, you outline services that are ill-adapted to the insurance company using technical jargon that the manager is too embarrassed to admit he doesn't understand. Feeling alienated, he becomes withdrawn and you don't know why. As a result, you fail to reach an agreement and the negotiation comes to nothing.

The key communication skills that any good negotiator needs to possess are: talking so that people will listen and understand you; listening so that people will give you all the information you require; asking the right kinds of questions; observing nonverbal signs; and being aware of meta-talk. All these skills are covered in detail in the first part of this chapter.

TALK SO PEOPLE WILL LISTEN

Words are the currency of any negotiation – the way you talk can make or break a discussion. In order to get your message across as effectively as possible, you need to ensure that you gain your listeners' attention and make your points clearly.

Before you speak, organize your thoughts. Make sure the points you make are sequential so people can easily follow what you are saying. If you are well prepared for the negotiation, you should be armed with succinct notes with key words highlighted for easy reference. However, once the negotiation is under way, you may have to react to unexpected information from the other party, in which case it is helpful to quickly jot down a short list of the key points they make, to help you formulate your response.

Gain the listeners' attention before you begin to talk. Don't speak over background noise – if necessary, pause until the floor is yours. Retain their attention by using a clear

voice loud enough for everyone to hear and making eye contact with your listeners so that you seem to be speaking directly to each of them. Be succinct; long-winded speeches turn people off. Stick to the point and avoid unrelated anecdotes. Above all, know when you have said enough, and stop.

Try to use language that will make your listeners feel positive both about you and about the negotiation. Here are some examples of phrases that are likely to be well received and therefore improve the negotiating climate:

- *I understand how strongly you feel.*
- *I want to hear everything that's on your mind.*
- *I like what you said a moment ago.*
- *We have resolved some issues and we're on our way to settlement.*
- *We have many objectives in common.*
- *I'll work very hard to get agreement on the remaining issues.*
- *I'm not in any hurry. I want us to conclude this meeting with an agreement we are both happy with.*

Avoid using the following phrases, which are likely to be poorly received and therefore damage the climate:

- *You're not trying to understand me.*
- *Don't interrupt me again.*
- *My position is absolutely firm. I'll never change it.*
- *You haven't got a leg to stand on.*
- *Didn't you even know that?*
- *I only have ten minutes left. Make up your mind!*

LISTEN SO PEOPLE WILL TALK

Listening is a skill that every negotiator should cultivate. With a little practice, it is possible to develop the ability to make the art of listening a part of the negotiating procedure.

The words "hear" and "listen" are often used as synonyms, but, in fact, they are not the same at all. As the communication expert Carol Grau says, "Active listening is all about the other person." If you are really listening effectively, you are not thinking of yourself and your own concerns while you are doing so. This is an essential negotiation skill. You won't understand the message if you don't give full attention to the speaker. Active listening is also crucial in preserving a good negotiating climate; if you show signs that you are not concentrating on what the other person is telling you, you risk creating an atmosphere of resentment and mistrust. However, by demonstrating that you are listening attentively, you will encourage the speaker to air any grievances he or she may have – these can then be dealt with openly.

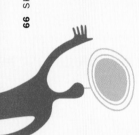

Through active listening, you communicate several things to the speaker that will keep your relations as warm and trusting as possible:

• *I'm interested in you, your ideas and your feelings.*
• *I respect your thoughts whether I agree or not.*
• *I'm a person you can talk to.*

Unfortunately, when we are anxious to conclude what seems to us a simple negotiation, we often display our impatience. Looking through papers on your desk, avoiding eye contact, interrupting the speaker, or looking at your watch are all signs of ineffective listening that will offend the other party as well as inhibit your ability to understand the implications of what they are saying. See the box below for some practical tips on how to listen effectively during negotiations.

ACTIVE LISTENING

Here are some ways to ensure that when someone speaks to you you're not just hearing the words, but seeking to understand the message:

- *Take time to listen. Do not try to rush the speaker.*

- *Give feedback, but not necessarily in words. Often a smile or nod of the head is enough to indicate nonverbally that you are paying attention.*

- *Force yourself to listen carefully for the message.*

- *Ask for clarification if the message is not clear.*

- *As soon as your mind begins to wander, refocus your attention on what the speaker is saying.*

- *Probe sensitively for additional information, lest you cause the speaker to withhold information he or she would otherwise reveal.*

- *Don't be critical and don't pass judgment. Instead, concentrate on what is being said, particularly if you are not interested in what the speaker is saying.*

- *Take careful note of the nonverbal signals you're receiving. Do you sense anxiety, tension, anger, mistrust? Can you respond in a way that reduces the negative feelings you're witnessing?*

- *Try not to start preparing your reply while the other person is talking. Make quick notes so you won't forget the point you're anxious to get across, but don't be distracted from listening and understanding the speaker's words and intent.*

- *Do not be tempted to give advice before the other person has finished what they are saying – the speaker wants to be understood, not advised, and will resent your interruption.*

ASKING THE RIGHT QUESTIONS

Questions serve a very important function in our negotiations – when used with mindfulness, discretion and good judgment, they can secure others' attention, maintain interest in the matter under discussion and direct the course that you want the conversation to take. We ask questions in order to establish the other party's objectives, to gain insights into the beliefs and assumptions they hold about the facts under discussion, and to provide us with the power to control the climate. Often, by asking the right questions, you can lead the other party toward the conclusion you desire.

When deciding whether to ask a question, think about what you hope it will achieve and consider the effect it is likely to have on the negotiating climate. A good way to do this is to think about each potential question in terms of objectives, needs and climate:

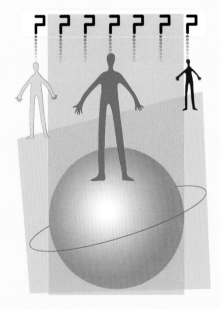

- *Objectives: What information do I hope to obtain by asking this question?*
- *Needs: Am I framing this question in a non-threatening way so as not to alarm the other party?*
- *Climate: If my question causes anxiety, what can I do to repair the breach?*

Always ensure that the purpose of your question is clear. During the negotiation itself, if the other party shows signs of anxiety in reaction to a question that you ask, you should act immediately to remedy this problem by withdrawing your query, or by rephrasing it in a way that renders it less threatening.

In formal negotiations, it is helpful to prepare your main questions – those to which the answers are vital to the negotiation process – in advance. In this way, you don't run the risk of forgetting to ask for an important piece of information. Knowing what you plan to ask enables you to move question by question to a close. It also allows you to listen attentively to what the other person is saying instead of thinking about what your next question should be. However, beware of relying too heavily on a list of prepared questions, as this can limit your flexibility. You may well have to react spontaneously to new scenarios thrown up in the course of the negotiation, which means you will also need to be able to frame constructive questions on the spot.

A useful approach to formulating questions, whether in advance or during a negotiation, is to consider the function that a question serves in the communication process. Five different functions of questions that can either help or hinder your negotiation efforts have been identified:

function 1: to gain attention
"How's your family?" / "Have you played golf recently?"
These openers serve as attention getters. Some cultures demand that a great deal of time be spent on opening questions. Part of the preparation for the negotiation should include research into the background of the parties so that these openings can be made relevant.

function 2: to seek information

"How much does it cost?"/"When will it be delivered?"

This form of questioning is designed to obtain the information necessary to move the discussion along, and ordinarily does not produce anxiety in the listener, unless he or she is suspicious of your motives in asking the question.

function 3: to give a negative message

"Are you a hypochondriac?"/"Are you having problems at home?"

This type of question is designed to give information rather than to receive it. Questions such as these might make the listener anxious or annoyed, because he or she suspects that the question is a means of expressing the questioner's negative opinion of him or her.

function 4: to start people thinking

"Have you ever considered…?"/"Are there any alternatives?"

These are questions that, when skillfully used, can move a

THE QUESTION MAP

Function 1 questions	Function 2 questions	Function 4 questions	Function 5 questions
(to gain attention)	(to get information)	(to stimulate thought)	(to close the deal)
1.	1.	1.	1.
2.	2.	2.	2.
3.	3.	3.	3.

Function 3 questions not used
(because they damage the climate; see above)

negotiation to a successful close. This type of question can put answers into the other person's mind. They can also stimulate creative thinking, for example: "If we used such and such a material, what kind of product would we get?"

function 5: to conclude the negotiation

"Are we all agreed?"/"Shall I draw up the contract?"

Knowing when a negotiation is complete and how to bring it to a close is a skill. You might recognize that you've made a sale of your product when the prospective purchaser asks whether it comes in purple or when he or she can take delivery, thus indicating that the fundamental issues have been settled. However, you need a good sense of timing to ask negotiation-closing questions, since they can cause resentment if posed before the other person feels the discussion is finished (see pp.84–7).

An alternative role for Function 5 questions is to keep the door open for future negotiations where a successful conclusion is not about to happen at the moment. For example, "When would it be convenient for you to see my associate who is an expert on the marketing of your product?" or, "I see that you are pressed for time today. Shall we continue our discussions on Wednesday of next week?"

With the question map (see opposite) in front of you, you can use questions to signpost the phases of your next negotiation. You will notice that Function 3 questions are missing from this map because they are likely to create a negative or hostile climate and therefore have no place in a positive negotiation.

READING NONVERBAL SIGNS

The conventional verbal skills of reading, writing, speaking and listening are only part of how we communicate in a negotiation. Far more revealing is nonverbal behaviour, which can tell us, for example, when our arguments are on target, whether the other parties find us believable, when things have gone sour or when we've arrived at a point of agreement sufficient to start closing the deal. The skilled negotiator therefore keeps his or her eyes and ears focused on the other person's mannerisms, facial expressions and gestures, all of which are important nonverbal clues to that person's thoughts and desires. Equally important is an awareness of and ability to control the nonverbal signs we transmit, allowing us to communicate positive nonverbal messages whenever possible.

We define nonverbal signs as any information which our senses perceive but which is not written or spoken. Therefore, everything we see, touch, smell and hear that is not structured as formal verbal input should be considered nonverbal information. nonverbal signs can be voluntary – for example, applauding to communicate approval. However, more often they are involuntary. Many involuntary gestures, such as frowning or tapping the table impatiently, that convey a negative message can be controlled with practice once we become aware of them (see Work Solution 8, p.75). Others, such as blushing, result from chemical reactions in our body that are largely beyond our control.

You can hone your ability to spot and analyze nonverbal signs by people-watching during your commute to and from work or at parties. Look out for physical clues as to what someone else is feeling or thinking. Remember, "gestures" are much more than simple body motions. Tension can be shown by any number of signs, such as tightening of the facial muscles or fidgeting. Facial expressions are an obvious means of nonverbal communication. Even the "poker face" – a total lack of expression – tells us that the other person does not want us to know anything about his or her feelings.

If you observe nonverbal signs that you find difficult to decipher, try to empathize with the other person. Consider

DECODING NONVERBAL BEHAVIOUR

There are some nonverbal communications that are warnings that the negotiation is not going well and that the other party is not ready for the close. The following is a short list of nonverbal signs to watch out for. They may indicate defensiveness, suspicion or doubtfulness, especially if they occur in clusters:

- *Not looking at you*
- *Arms crossed*
- *Feet/body pointing toward exit*
- *Touching/rubbing nose*
- *Hand over mouth*

Some non-reassuring, bored or evaluating nonverbal signs:

- *Doodling*
- *Drumming on table*
- *Hand to face gestures*
- *Chewing earpiece of glasses*
- *Stroking chin*

Then there are nonverbal signs that reassure you that the negotiation is going well and that you will soon be able to close the deal:

- *Nodding approval*
- *Sounds of approval, such as "uh-huh"*
- *Leaning forward*
- *Smiling*

how you would have to feel to make those signs. Ask the person discreet questions, such as "Are you comfortable with that arrangement?", that will help you to discover the emotions behind their gestures and make them feel more at ease.

When watching out for nonverbal signs, remember that a single, isolated gesture may have no significance. For example, arms folded across the chest may simply mean that the person is cold rather than defiant. A cluster of gestures, however, should always be taken seriously.

Even when we are adept at reading the nonverbal signs of others, we are often less aware of our own. Work Solution 8, opposite, gives guidance on how to analyze your nonverbal signs. Being aware of the messages you are giving out can help you to control your gestures and limit them to neutral or positive signs. During a negotiation, every so often take a few seconds to ask yourself the following questions:

- *What am I feeling right now?*
- *Am I expressing these feelings through nonverbal signs?*
- *Am I happy for the other party to pick up on these emotions, or should I be trying to control the nonverbal signs I am giving out because they are negative?*

However, it is important to avoid trying too hard to control all our own nonverbal behaviour in an attempt to camouflage our true selves. If we try to use gestures or facial expressions to manipulate rather than communicate, we run the risk of appearing false. The simplest way to alter your gestures is first to change how you feel. The gestures will then change automatically because they are natural.

WORK SOLUTION 8

Mirror, mirror on the wall

In order to be aware of and control the nonverbal signs you give out during negotiations, you need to get used to spotting them. A good way to do this is to replay one of your recent negotiations in your mind. Imagine that you are back in that meeting – opposite you there is a mirror on the wall in which you can observe yourself without anyone else noticing. Now imagine that you are watching yourself taking part in the negotiation; examine your own nonverbal behaviour by running through the checklist below. With practice, you can learn to do these checks very quickly in your mind while you are actually in a real negotiation – in this way, you can act as your own invisible mirror, keeping an eye on your nonverbal signs and making any necessary corrections immediately.

1. Check your posture to ensure that stooping shoulders are not revealing your flagging spirits.

2. Check your hands to be sure you are not wringing them in despair or fear.

3. Check that your arms and legs are not crossed in a display of closed-mindedness, defiance or hostility.

4. Check the placement of your body on your seat – does it suggest an attitude of attentiveness toward or rejection of the speaker?

5. Check your face, the most telling part of your anatomy. Start with your eyebrows and eyes, then your lips, your mouth and jaw, to be sure that you are not a picture of fear, anxiety, scepticism, hostility, anger, superiority, disdain, and so on.

6. Take a deep breath and let go of the negative emotions revealed to you by this body tour. A fairer, more open-looking you will emerge when the emotion changes.

UNDERSTANDING META-TALK

During negotiations, we often try to protect ourselves by being indirect – this is known as meta-talk. For example, we may say "honestly" or "I want to be perfectly frank" to cover up the fact that we are not being entirely truthful. Insight into meta-talk allows us to avoid using seemingly innocuous phrases that may make the other party feel suspicious and helps us to discover meanings that the speaker is attempting to hide or obscure.

An awareness of meta-talk can often give a valuable insight into somebody else's motivations. For example, if your delivery of component parts is late and the shipping agent says, "Don't worry, you'll get your shipment", you can infer that something is wrong and that he or she is playing for time. As a general rule, when you hear "don't worry" you need to start pressing the other person to tell you the real story and outline what is being done to correct the problem.

Work Solution 9 (see p.79) gives advice on how to analyze your own speech for meta-talk. You also can train yourself to recognize the significance of other people's meta-talk. When you are taking part in a discussion, try regularly asking yourself, "What does the speaker *really* mean by that?" Study the following categories of meta-talk and listen out for their use next time you are in a negotiation.

softeners

Softeners are attempts to put the listener in a positive frame of mind. The speaker may say, "I'm sure someone as intelligent as you will see that this makes sense", or "What is your expert opinion?" The hidden meaning is, "I've been extra nice to you, now you should return the favour by agreeing with my proposal." Never let flattery (see pp.122–3) distract you from your own needs and objectives – instead, try asking yourself, "Why is the speaker so anxious to get me to agree to this?"

foreboders

These set the stage for bad news. If the other person says "Don't worry about me" or "Nothing is wrong" (accompanied by visible signs of anxiety), they are alerting you to the fact that something is wrong. If somebody uses a foreboder, rather than allowing it to make you feel nervous too, gently

I KNOW WHAT YOU REALLY MEAN

The perceptive listener can learn much more than the speaker would like. Sometimes the intended meaning of words is opposite of what is being said. A knowledge of meta-talk provides important information about what the speaker really means.

Before I forget... / *Here comes the real message*

As you well know / *Now you won't admit you don't know*

Everybody says I'm a great manager / *I think I'm a hopeless manager*

It's none of my business, but... / *I'm making it my business*

I would never lie to you / *A red flag! I may be lying now*

You didn't know that? / *You must be pretty stupid*

Off the top of my head / *I don't know, but I'll speak as if I do*

The matter is closed! / *I won't tolerate any discussion!*

I'll do my best / *If it doesn't work out, I warned you*

First the good news / *You can expect the bad stuff to follow*

ask them to explain exactly what it is that is making them anxious. That way the problem is brought out into the open and you can look for solutions together.

continuers

These are attempts to get the listener to disclose his or her thoughts. "Go on, and then?", "That's very good", and "Now you're talking" are all examples of continuers. Disclosure can be helpful in a business negotiation if you are trying to establish trust. But don't fall prey to somebody's effort to get you to reveal bits of information before you are ready to do so.

convincers

Convincers are used to try to persuade you of the logic of what the speaker secretly knows is an illogical argument. "Everybody is doing it" is used to justify an unwise course of action. "Anyone can follow my reasoning" implies that if you can't, there's something wrong with you! Refuse to be taken in and continue to point out calmly the flaws in the speaker's argument until they revise their position.

strokers

A stroker is a response to an appeal for reassurance. For example, if someone asks, "Did I go too far with that suggestion about stock options?", you might answer with a stroker purely in the interests of a good climate: "I really liked your suggestion." However, if you add, "But it hasn't got a chance of even getting a hearing", you will have negated your reassuring words with the verbal eraser, "but" and the other person will realize that your compliment was insincere.

WORK SOLUTION 9

A plain-speaking campaign

There are lots of reasons for using meta-talk – we may want to avoid a dispute, soften unpleasant news or purposely mislead. However, meta-talk should be avoided in negotiations, because it inhibits clear communication. And remember, if you can see through the other person's meta-talk, they can probably see through yours! Being direct, although it might not be easier, is more honest and ultimately creates a far better negotiating climate.

The following exercise teaches you to analyze your own speech patterns for misleading phrases. Before long, you will be aware of the temptation to resort to meta-talk and learn to resist it and say something more direct instead.

1. Begin by recording some of your telephone conversations or printing out some of your recent transactional e-mails. Play back the conversations or read through the e-mails, looking out for any seemingly harmless little phrases that obscured your meaning. Make a list of the meta-talk phrases you seem to be in the habit of using regularly; note how often you resort to using them during the course of a typical conversation or e-mail.

2. Think about what the hidden meaning was behind your words on the various occasions when you used the phrases on your list. Ask yourself which of the phrases may have a damaging effect on your communication by distancing you from the other person or making them suspicious of your true motives. How could you have got your message across more directly in each case?

3. Next time you are in a negotiation, be mindful of the damaging meta-talk phrases you usually resort to and try to avoid using them. Instead, think of what you want to say and drum up the courage to say it directly, without subterfuge. To force yourself to abandon your bad meta-talk habits, you could even charge yourself a small fine every time you use meta-talk and give the money to charity.

PERSUASION

Persuasion implies subtly imposing your will on the other side, prevailing over objections and bringing the other person round to your way of thinking. Most of us feel resentful when someone uses clumsy, antagonistic methods of persuasion on us. However, we usually respond positively to persuasion techniques that aim to help solve our problems. A skilled negotiator therefore uses subtle, constructive persuasion techniques that seek to satisfy the needs of both parties. This requires an understanding of the other person's needs and an ability to frame our proposals in a way that shows we appreciate those needs.

Below are some of the main methods of persuasion. Some can be very useful during negotiations, others can be destructive and should be avoided or used with care. If you sense that the other person resents the persuasion technique you have chosen, examine whether your efforts to persuade are really an attempt to manipulate. Try another, more gentle technique and stay focused on the needs of all the parties involved.

logical argument

The use of a well presented, logical argument is a persuasion technique that is generally greeted with respect, rather than hostility. However, it can be used only when you know you have a watertight case – for example, if you are trying to secure a distribution deal for a new product and you are able to provide solid market research proving that demand is high and good profit margins are guaranteed. If there are any flaws in your argument, you will lose all credibility.

appeal to a strongly felt emotion

Many efforts to persuade are based on exploiting a strong emotion, such as pride or fear, in the listener. For example, an estate agent may appeal to a client's pride by saying, "This house is perfect for someone with your high standing in the community", or an insurance salesperson may frighten a potential customer with dire warnings about what might happen if they don't take out a policy. This tactic should be used with caution. Flattery can make the other party wary of your motives, while playing on the listener's fears can cause him or her to identify you with the threat and react with hostility.

reliance on power/coercion

Reminding the other party of your power over them and using coercion techniques to bend them to your will can sometimes be effective. For example, if you are negotiating

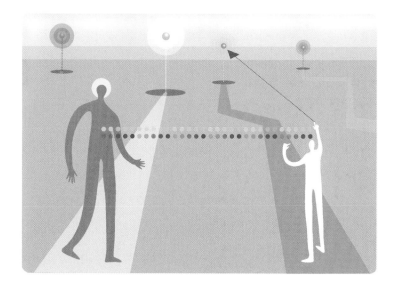

the purchase of a new product from a supplier, you could remind them that you are one of their main customers, insinuating that if you do not get the terms you want, you might withdraw your business altogether. However, beware – such tactics may encourage retaliation or alienate the other party beyond repair. If you do resort to this method, make sure that you exercise your power in a way that will not undermine the respect, trust and acceptance of the other party.

seeking a compromise

By being seen to seek a compromise on the main issue under discussion, you can create a climate of cooperation, increasing your chances of persuading the listener to give in to some of your demands on other issues. First, get the other person to express their concerns so you can focus on resolving them. This constructive method of persuasion promotes an "everybody wins" climate. It is useful in negotiations where there are several issues, for example where the central issue is one of price in a sales deal – you may be prepared to compromise on price, but not on delivery and invoicing arrangements.

offering a trade-off

People naturally feel an obligation to reciprocate favours they have received. For example, a salesperson may offer to waive a delivery charge. The other person is then expected to reciprocate the apparent concession, perhaps by agreeing to the price demanded. To use this technique, you have to be confident that the rewards will more than make up for your "concession". However, you do need to be subtle – if the other person feels they are being manipulated your tactics may backfire.

WORK SOLUTION 10

Practise persuasion techniques

In order to use a range of persuasion techniques effectively, and, very importantly, to gain a feel for which techniques to use in different negotiating situations, you need to hone your persuasion skills. For each of the following imaginary negotiation scenarios, think about how each of the five persuasion techniques described on pages 80–82 might be used. Enlist the help of a colleague or friend to act out the imaginary negotiations with you, taking it in turns to play the role of the persuader. Act each scenario out several times, starting with a different persuasion technique every time – use as many of the techniques as you can. Remember, you may have to change technique in the middle of a negotiation if you sense that the climate is deteriorating. After applying several techniques to a scenario, you and your partner should assess how successful each tactic was and decide which would be the best one to use in a similar, real-life situation.

Scenario 1

You sell advertising space for a national trade magazine. You are trying to convince one of your regular customers to take out a full-page ad in your next issue. The customer usually only buys the much cheaper quarter-page advertisements, but you know that her company is currently promoting a major new product.

Scenario 2

You are an event organiser trying to persuade a caterer who relies on your business to provide the food for a very large function (a three-day national conference) for a lower fee per head than usual.

Scenario 3

You are trying to persuade one of your most valued employees to take on new responsibilities, but you don't want to offer him a pay rise, as your salary budget is very tight this year. You know that he will probably balk at the idea of working longer hours for the same pay, especially as he has just become a father.

DECISION TIME

Knowing when and how to bring a negotiation to a close and on what terms requires sensitivity and skill. You need to decide whether you or the other party should make the final offer and what the terms should be, as well as judging the right moment for moving to the agreement phase.

Both parties have come to the negotiation with needs and objectives, each of which will have to be satisfactorily dealt with before it's time to close. Any proposed solution must be mutually acceptable if a long-lasting agreement and continuing good relationship is to be the outcome.

The agreement phase is triggered by one party putting a final offer on the table. The timing of this stage of the negotiation is crucial. It can be damaging to let talks drag on long after a satisfactory agreement could have been reached while both parties indulge in endless haggling. However, it can be just as dangerous to initiate the close before the other party

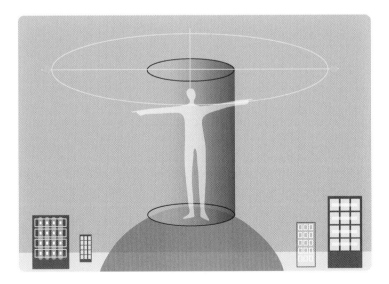

is ready – the risk is that he or she, feeling pressured, will ask for an adjournment to "think about it" and may never return. For clues about whether the agreement phase is approaching, watch out for the other party's verbal and nonverbal signs – if the signs suggest rejection, reserve, suspicion or another negative emotion, you need to deal with that first. Final decisions cannot be reached until a positive climate has been restored. However, if the other party is showing signs of acceptance and readiness – for example, nodding, making sounds of approval, such as "uh-huh", leaning forward, or smiling – it is probably time to seal the deal.

Each negotiation is unique, and there are no firm rules as to who should make the final offer. However, it is more usual for the party who instituted the negotiation to be the one to make the closing move. Whether or not that is you, you can demonstrate your readiness to complete the negotiation by asking a question that calls for a positive closing response, such as "When would you like delivery?" or "How many dozen would you like and in what colour?"

If you decide to make the final offer yourself, first stop and take some time to reflect on what that offer should be. See Work Solution 11 on page 87 for advice on how to use this pause for reflection constructively. Due deliberation is crucial at this stage – if you allow yourself to be rushed into making the final offer without thinking it through properly, you may later regret it, perhaps wishing in retrospect that you had held out for more money or better terms. However, you will lose all credibility if you go back on your offer once the

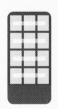

other party has accepted it. So before you make your move, ask yourself whether your offer will meet all your needs and those of the other party. For example, if you are a supplier negotiating the sale of raw materials to a customer and you have lowered your original asking price, make sure that the price you are about to propose meets your objectives. Is the customer likely to be satisfied with the new price, even though it is more than he or she was initially hoping to pay? Are you confident that your company will be able to fulfil the terms of delivery you are proposing?

The same rule of caution applies if the other party makes the final offer and you have to decide whether or not to accept it. Remember that the outcome is only successful if both parties come away satisfied. Never agree to an offer without thinking it through because you are tired or you sense that the other party is rushing you into a conclusion.

Intuition plays an important role in this decision-making process. After you have examined rationally all the elements, you may find that it is your feeling about the situation – how reliable you sense the other party is, whether you suspect that he or she might be willing to compromise further – that guides your final decision.

Once an agreement has been reached, go over the terms of the deal verbally to make sure that both parties are clear and agree on what has been decided. Arrange for the agreement to be confirmed in writing as soon as possible. Whether you or the other party is responsible for drawing up the contract to be signed, make sure you make detailed notes about exactly what was agreed upon immediately after the meeting while everything that was discussed is still fresh in your mind.

WORK SOLUTION 11

Look before you leap

As the negotiation reaches its close, the moment has come for one last pause for reflection. Always take as much time as you need to weigh up what your final offer should be, or to decide whether to accept the other party's offer. Never rush into proposing or accepting a deal – it is better to give yourself a chance to think things through, even if that means excusing yourself from the negotiation for a while, than to find yourself wishing later that you had done things differently. The other party will understand the wisdom of your taking time to examine the situation, and will probably seize the opportunity to do the same thing. Remember, if the other person is a good negotiator, he or she will be keen for everyone to walk away from the encounter satisfied with the conclusion.

1. As a means of clarifying your thoughts, draw up a balance sheet on which you list the pros and cons of each of the courses of action now open to you.

2. Whether you are making the final offer or deciding whether to accept an offer made by the other party, make a list of all your needs and objectives and also what you think those of the other party are. Does the offer on the table satisfy all these needs and objectives? Have any been left unsatisfied that might cause problems later on, threatening the long-term success of the deal? For example, is there any danger that one of the parties will go away feeling so resentful about a concession made that he or she may even terminate the agreement at some point in the future? If so, the final offer needs to be rethought to rectify this.

3. Make absolutely sure that neither of you are about to agree to terms you might not be able to fulfil. Go through the proposed deal point by point asking yourself, "Am I sure that I/the other party can afford to pay this price/meet this delivery schedule/fulfil this production brief, and so on?" If you have any doubts, now is the time to raise them!

chapter 3

NEGOTIATING OBSTACLES

If negotiations always ran smoothly, you would not be reading this book. Adhering to an "everybody wins" philosophy, being guided by the elements of the Foundation and displaying the skills outlined in the previous chapter will all help you to achieve your objectives. However, you will still encounter problems along the way. The skilled negotiator views these as obstacles to be overcome rather than impenetrable barriers to further progress.

In this chapter, we will look at how to deal with some of the most common of these negotiation obstacles, such as manipulation, anger and misused power. We learn how to recognize the problem – for example, how we spot the first signs of irritation either in ourselves or in others or how we realize that we are wasting time on a minor issue. Having identified the obstacle, we explore ways of hurdling it in order to set the negotiation back on course.

THE POWER STRUGGLE

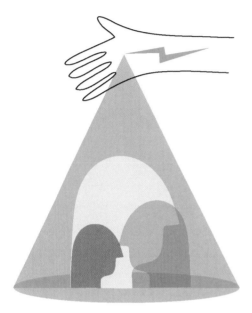

When we use the term power in the context of a negotiation, we are referring to an individual's capacity to dominate. The exercise of power can evoke strong emotions – at best, admiration, respect and compliance, at worst, fear, hostility, rejection or retaliation.

We can usually infer how much power someone has by looking at the hierarchical map of the organization for which he or she works. However, power is not always linked to a person's job title – an individual who combines a strong knowledge of the business he or she represents with well-honed negotiating skills can wield great personal power whatever their position. The balance of power can also vary from negotiation to negotiation, even if the same two people are present on each occasion. In any given discussion, the person who stands to gain the most or lose the least from the process holds the most power.

If we know that we hold the power in a negotiation, we should be careful to use it subtly to maintain a positive negotiating climate. Power should never be used to intimidate others, but instead to make them feel respected and valued. Bear in mind that people who consciously seek to demonstrate their power are often perceived as arrogant.

Unfortunately, some negotiators try to use their power to humiliate the other party in an attempt to coerce him or her into an agreement. Needless to say, such behaviour can be extremely damaging to the negotiating climate. Next time you are in a negotiation, look out for the following common forms of the misuse of power:

- *The undisguised use of gestures (such as raised eyebrow and chin) and tone of voice that announce haughtiness or disdain. The use of any other nonverbal messages that express dismissive feelings.*
- *The use of strategies and tactics designed to disadvantage the other parties, resulting in a negative climate.*
- *The use of questions that create anxiety in the other party, for example, "Why did you…?" or "Why didn't you…?"*
- *The failure to listen attentively to what is being said and a tendency to interrupt the speaker before he or she has finished.*
- *The use of technical terms or jargon, without explanation, to people who have no prior knowledge of the industry or business with which these terms are associated.*
- *The use of power deliberately to undermine others' esteem or safety and security needs through public criticism.*

If you perceive that someone is abusing their power in a negotiation, you need to tackle the abuser as quickly as possible in order to restore a positive climate. Remember that it is the person misusing their power who is diminished by their own behaviour. Demonstrate your self-assurance and refusal to be intimidated or undermined – if you can calmly turn a negative climate into a positive one you will, in effect, seize the power and be able to use it constructively.

MANIPULATION

Manipulation involves using various tactics to manoeuvre the other party into doing something you want them to do, preferably without their noticing what is happening. There is something of the manipulator in every negotiator.

There are many positive forms of manipulation – efforts to smooth ruffled feathers, bring about a reconciliation or resolve a conflict can often be viewed as manipulative. There is also an aspect of manipulation in taking control of the climate in order to keep it positive, paying attention to the needs of the other party, and persuading them, through the use of our skills, to a consideration of our point of view. If all this is done to create a winning solution for all parties, this form of manipulation can be an integral part of successful negotiating. For example, a salesperson knows that if you overload the customer with choices, you are likely to confuse him or her and make a decision more difficult. Making three or four options available is a positive manipulative device to facilitate the process for both parties. The customer always can ask to see additional merchandise if necessary.

Negative forms of manipulation tend be used by negotiators who are thinking only of their own interests, rather than those of both parties. Very often attempts to manipulate involve instilling a sense of urgency. For example, a broker may try to rush you into buying shares by saying, "This is the time to invest in this company. There's a very small window. By Friday you won't be able to buy in!" In such a situation, if there is not enough data for you to make an educated evaluation, refuse to allow yourself to be manipulated.

The key to dealing with manipulation is recognizing what is going on. When someone tries to get you to do something for his or her benefit at your expense – perhaps by using the hurry-up tactic or flattery – and you don't realize it, you are being manipulated. You are no longer being manipulated if you understand what is happening. It may even be advantageous to go along with the manipulator if, in doing so, you will advance the negotiation. For example, your boss might tell you that they want you to take on more responsibility because you are their most valued employee and they have great faith in your abilities. You can turn this attempt at manipulation through flattery to your advantage by thanking your boss for the compliment and pointing out that, as their most valued employee, you feel you are entitled to a raise.

ANGER AND CONFRONTATION

Angry behaviour during a negotiation can range from stony silence to an outburst of harsh words. The angry person may insult, demean or even physically threaten others. nonverbal signs of anger are hard to disguise – the muscles of the face tighten, the complexion reddens or goes pale, and the person may push their chair away from the table or even leave the room. Such confrontations can have an extremely detrimental effect on the negotiating climate. If we are to save the negotiation and the continuing, long-term relationship between the parties, it is vital that we deal with anger – our own or other people's – quickly and effectively.

However, occasionally a confrontation during a negotiation can be positive. Confrontation can help to bring any sticking points to the fore, allowing both parties to devote their energy to addressing those issues. For example, the directors of a large corporation held a meeting with their lawyer to try to get him to reduce an agreed-upon fee. The directors were deliberately provocative, testing the waters to see whether the lawyer could be coerced into a reduction. The lawyer was furious at this attempt to go back on a previous agreement, and he exploded in justifiable anger. As a result, the directors realized that to continue to haggle over the fee would damage the relationship beyond repair and agreed to honour the lawyer's demands. This confrontation, dramatic as it was, was thus satisfactorily concluded and the lawyer–client relationship was preserved.

If you find yourself faced with someone else's anger in a negotiation, sometimes the best thing to do is not to respond immediately. For the good of the negotiation, it is generally advisable to sidestep any personal attacks and focus on the issues being discussed. Your ability to stay calm can often shame the other person into controlling their temper. Suggest that you each make a list of difficult points and then agree on the order in which they should be discussed. The very act of writing a list slows down the action and allows the anger to dissipate. If the anger can't be contained, have an intermission or arrange to continue another day. Next time you meet with that individual, appoint a neutral person to be a moderator in case the anger erupts again.

If you suspect that your own words or actions are responsible for a confrontation, run through what has happened in your mind. Were you feeling hostile toward the other person, or irritated by them? If so, you may have let these feelings show without realizing it. Examine the other party's speech and nonverbal signs. Is that person clearly on the defensive, suggesting that he or she feels attacked? If you decide that you are indeed the cause of the confrontation, you must move rapidly to put things right. Make a conscious effort to be conciliatory – ensure that your nonverbal signs are friendly, rather than aggressive

RELIEVING TENSION
The Chinese therapy of acupressure teaches that we can relieve tension by applying pressure to special points on our skin to unblock the flow of qi, or life energy. Find the spot one finger's width below the crease on the inside of your wrist. Press your thumb on the skin directly in line with your little finger. Hold the pressure for around a minute or until you feel calm. If tension is making you nauseous, press your thumb firmly between the two bones on your inner forearm, three fingers' width below the wrist crease, for 30 to 60 seconds.

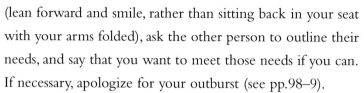

(lean forward and smile, rather than sitting back in your seat with your arms folded), ask the other person to outline their needs, and say that you want to meet those needs if you can. If necessary, apologize for your outburst (see pp.98–9).

Anger is not always uncontrolled. Frequently an angry display is exaggerated for specific purposes. The seemingly angry person may not be angry at all, but has calculated that the display will cow you, make you concede some points, unnerve you or put an end to any aggression you may be showing. He or she may display anger to show the serious-ness of their position. This may be their method of getting you to examine the reasonableness of your position, or to make you feel threatened, embarrassed, inadequate or uncomfortable. nonverbal signs, because they are very diffi-cult to fake, can be helpful clues as to whether anger is gen-uine. If the nonverbal signs of anger are missing, the other person is probably using anger as a tactic. Similarly, ask your-self whether this outburst is likely to be damaging to both parties. If so, it is genuine – no one deliberately damages their own position. However, if the confrontation is likely to ben-efit the angry person at your expense, it is probably manipu-lative. In this case, stay calm and don't add fuel to the fire. Instead of responding in kind, wait until the apparent anger subsides, and coax the negotiation back on course.

If, while you are in a negotiation, you can feel your own anger rising, you need to suppress it before it can escalate and result in a confrontation. A simple breathing exercise might help you to bring your anger under control – see Work Solution 12, opposite. Concentrate on dealing with the other party's needs rather than dwelling on your angry feelings.

WORK SOLUTION 12

Deep breaths

At times of stress, our breathing becomes rapid and shallow, which sets in motion a vicious circle of increased anxiety and agitation that, left unchecked, often leads to an angry confrontation. However, the good news is that we have the power to control our breathing and, in so doing, avoid losing our temper. Practise the following breathing exercise regularly, so that it comes naturally. This will make it easier to put it into action when you feel the first signs of irritation in the middle of a negotiation.

1. Pause to focus on your breathing. Is it irregular and fast? Or is it deep, even and slow? Place one hand on your upper chest and the other on your stomach, just below your ribs. Take a fairly deep breath and look to see which of your hands moves first and moves more. If it is your upper hand, you need to alter your breathing pattern so that you breathe with your diaphragm rather than with your upper chest. This will enable you to breathe more deeply.

2. Expand your diaphragm fully to take an in-breath. Exhale gently, slowly and fully through pursed lips. Imagine there is a small candle just in front of your mouth. And imagine that the candle represents the negotiation. Your task is to breathe out so gently that you do not extinguish the candle. Feel the frustrations that have built up inside you being purged from your body along with the breath.

3. When you have completed your exhalation, breathe in freely and fully. Then exhale again in the same way as before.

4. Repeat this cycle of gentle, full inhalation and exhalation for as long as you can. You should begin to feel much calmer after approximately 15 cycles.

MAKING MISTAKES

As we know, a good climate is a vital part of any successful negotiation – this means that there are times when we need to apologize for our mistakes. Infractions can range from irritating lapses, such as being late for a meeting, to grave errors, such as unintentionally supplying erroneous data in a report.

Sadly, some people cannot bear to extend an apology, even when the gesture is clearly called for, believing that to say they're sorry would weaken their image, cause them to be rejected or rob them of others' esteem. Such individuals would rather stonewall and let the climate suffer than apologize. When this happens, the satisfactory outcome of the negotiation is threatened and both parties usually lose out.

If you have made a mistake for which you feel that you need to apologize (see box, opposite, for advice on how to reach that decision), try to strike while the iron's hot. An apology made quickly will be much less embarrassing for you and much better received by the other party than one made long after the error was committed.

Before you speak, take a moment to calm your nerves and think about the best way to present your apology. It is not always easy to say you're sorry, and the prospect of doing so often makes us feel anxious, which can lead us to phrase the apology somewhat clumsily. Yet the way in which you say it is as important as the gesture itself. When making your apology, remember that the apologizer who is sincere is usually forgiven. What doesn't work is an apology that begins, "I was guilty, but … ." Here,

When you find yourself in a negotiation in which you are aware that you might have done something wrong, you need to weigh up the situation and decide whether you should say you're sorry for the good of the negotiating climate. Ask yourself the following questions:

• *Have I made a mistake?*
• *Will an apology improve a damaged climate?*
• *Will my failure to apologize lead to a deadlock, or worse still, to the premature end of the negotiation?*

"but" is a verbal eraser that renders your apology almost worthless. Bear in mind that your aim should not be to gain sympathy – keep the apology brief but genuine, and then get on with business. Others will ultimately respect you for having had the courage to say you're sorry. In fact, an apology often has the effect of completely disarming someone who might have been looking to get even.

If you are the recipient of an apology, you have certain obligations to fulfil. It is helpful for the person who risked extending the apology if you acknowledge it with a few words of appreciation prior to the resumption of negotiations. The other party will be grateful for any reciprocal offering that allows him or her to save face. Similarly, if you receive an apology that is oblique, try to be generous. The offering may be the other person's self-conscious attempt to do the right thing, but all that he or she is capable of.

If you are feeling such strong anger or hurt that you are inclined to reject an apology, take a pause for reflection and review your objectives. A positive climate can be restored if you allow it – swallow your pride!

BLIND ALLEYS

Digression and over-concentration on irrelevant or peripheral issues are among the most common barriers to progress in negotiations. These tendencies – which lead the discussion into blind alleys, from where it can go nowhere – hinder us in achieving our objectives, especially if time is tight, and can even cause the negotiation to fail completely.

There are several factors that can send a discussion down a blind alley. For example, if one or both parties is poorly prepared for the negotiation, time will be wasted going over information that the participants could easily have studied before the meeting.

An ill-defined agenda is also often responsible for unnecessary debate. It is vital, therefore, that both parties draw up a list of points to be discussed in advance of the negotiation, and agree on the order in which the points are to be tackled and the relative importance that should be accorded to each one (see pp.52–3). Many issues can be settled relatively easily. You may want to tackle those first and then move on to the more difficult issues. Alternatively, if time is very tight, you might prefer to go over the most important issues first, so that you can be sure that those will be dealt with before you run out of time. If any minor issues are left uncovered, you may be able to arrange to discuss them on another day or by telephone or e-mail later. Although an agenda should be flexible rather than prescriptive, without at least a basic plan it can be very difficult to control the direction of the negotiation and a great deal of time may be lost discussing minor issues at the expense of the major ones.

Another hold-up we often face is a lack of flexibility on the part of one of the negotiators. If one person adopts an entrenched position and flatly refuses to compromise on an issue, it can become impossible to move the discussion forward. This is why it is so important to bear in mind the needs (see pp.18–23) of all the parties throughout the negotiation – there is simply no point in sticking stubbornly to your demands on a minor issue if, in doing so, you cause the whole negotiation to derail and you all come away with no agreement.

Many negotiations fail to reach a satisfactory conclusion because time has been wasted on red herrings – extraneous issues that are irrelevant to the discussion. A red herring may

be introduced by one of the parties as a deliberate diversionary tactic or even as an attempt to sabotage the negotiation, or it may be a topic that is brought up innocently – either way, you need to be able to recognize when a red herring is threatening a negotiation.

As the discussion moves on to each new point, quickly ask yourself whether the topic is relevant to the negotiation, whether it is of major or minor importance, and how much time you think you should be allotting to its discussion. If you feel that time is being wasted on irrelevant subjects, you need to act to set the discussion back on course as quickly as possible. You could politely suggest setting a time-limit, by saying something such as, "With time being short, how about we agree to resolve this issue in the next ten minutes so that we can move on to another point?" If time is running out, you might suggest that you abandon the debate on the peripheral subject for now and move on to the next issue on the agenda. However, so as not to offend the person who introduced the red herring, try to avoid dismissing the topic altogether, perhaps by asking, "Do you have any objections to us getting the major points on the agenda out of the way now, and then coming back to this subject if we have some time left at the end?" Remember that what seems irrelevant to you might be crucial to the other person. Your question gives the other party a chance to explain why that topic is important to them if necessary, while encouraging them to get (or keep) to the point.

WORK SOLUTION 13

Keep an eye on the clock

Although not all negotiations are time-sensitive (some drag on for years before they reach a resolution), for the most part, negotiators are constrained by time and should develop the skill of staying focused on getting the job done. If you are in a negotiation that is stagnating, how do you overcome the hold-up and keep the discussion moving? Before your next time-sensitive negotiation, run through the following tips, and try to apply them when necessary.

1. Plan the agenda for the negotiation in advance, preferably in collaboration with the other party, and decide roughly how much time should be allowed for the discussion of each item.

2. Appoint a timekeeper to alert you when time is running out on the issue you're discussing. Remember that sometimes it will not be possible to stick exactly to your schedule, but the very act of checking how much time has been spent and how much is left will help prevent digressions.

3. If the discussion becomes bogged down by a particular issue, take steps to tackle the sticking point. If everyone agrees that it is an irrelevant or unimportant point, suggest that it is dropped or put to one side until the major issues have been agreed upon. If it is an important point, suggest leaving it temporarily while other ground is covered and coming back to it later when all the parties may be in a more positive frame of mind.

4. If the discussion seems to be going round in circles, it might simply be because everyone is tired. You may actually speed things up by suggesting that you all take a short break for refreshments, after which the parties can return to the negotiation with clearer heads and talks can continue more efficiently.

REJECTION

During the course of any negotiation, there can be numerous rejections of offers and counter-offers. If your offers do not meet the objectives or needs of the other party you can expect rejections to follow. In some cases you may even fail to reach any kind of agreement.

Bear in mind that needs include esteem needs (see p.21) and that these should be taken seriously if we are to avoid rejection. For example, the owner of a small delicatessen in a business district, catering mainly to take-out customers, with a few tables and chairs provided for those with time to eat on the premises, was negotiating the buy-out of his business. He had come to agreements with the prospective buyer on prices for the fixtures, provisions, utensils, and so on, although not without intense bargaining back and forth. Finally, the purchaser said, "Throw in the tables and chairs – which I probably won't use anyway – and we have a deal." To which the owner replied sharply, "NO! I would rather take them away and store them in my basement than give them to you." The seller in this case had suffered an attack on his esteem needs. He had taken every counter offer for his property personally and the final blow was the buyer's failure to recognize the value of his tables and chairs. As a result, he rejected the buyer's final offer and the negotiation collapsed.

It is never pleasant to be on the receiving end of a rejection in a negotiation, but if it happens to us, we need to keep the door open for future business with the other party. Whenever you experience a rejection of your offer, ensure that you remain calm and polite. The burden is on you to demonstrate the merits of your position.

In order to avoid rejection in the first place, we must make sure that what we are offering meets the other party's needs and objectives as well as our own. The more attention we pay to justifying our offers and counter-offers, based on the objectives and needs of both parties, the greater the chance of acceptance and the more likely the eventual success of the negotiation.

For example, in the negotiation between the deli owner and the potential buyer, a deal could have been reached if the buyer had realized that she had failed to fulfil the seller's esteem needs as soon as her offer was rejected. She could then have repaired the damage by apologizing and offering to buy the tables and chairs if the price fell within her budget.

WHAT WENT WRONG?

After a failed negotiation, take a pause to consider whether you could have done anything differently. Did you pay proper attention to the other party's needs and objectives? Did you ask questions to elicit the facts or assumptions underpinning their position, or did you simply justify your own position? Did you do your utmost to maintain a positive climate at all times? If, even though the negotiation has failed, you can be confident that you have handled the situation well throughout, take heart. Remind yourself that the fault may not be yours – or anyone's, for that matter.

chapter 4

NEGOTIATING WITH DIFFICULT PEOPLE

Of the various aspects of successful negotiation, dealing with difficult people is, for many of us, the most challenging. Most people can happily master techniques such as organizing agendas and determining objectives, but, faced with someone who is displaying extreme emotion or being antagonistic, they will quickly lose confidence. Even the most skilled negotiator may find it hard to cope with

negative, disarming and manipulative behaviour.

In this chapter we will learn how to deal calmly with various types of highly charged behaviour and develop skills for keeping the focus of all parties on the aims of the negotiation itself. We will examine different behavioural tendencies (in ourselves and others) and learn to look for and encourage the positive qualities in any individual. While it is important to be able to identify negative behaviour, in order to stop it derailing the negotiation, we will also see how harmful it can be to label people based on a single aspect of their personality.

PEELING OFF THE LABELS

We have all had to deal with difficult people. There is no doubt that many unsuccessful negotiations owe their failure to the damaging behaviour of these individuals. However, negotiations can also suffer if we allow our preconceived ideas about other people to interfere with our dealings with them. If we brand someone as a bully or a liar, it gives us someone to blame if the negotiation doesn't work out. A more productive approach is to consider how we perceive other people and ensure that we do so with an open mind.

Inevitably, when we first meet someone we form an impression of them. Over time, that impression may become a fixed way of perceiving them (for example, "He's aggressive", "She's indecisive"). We consider it to be an eternal truth about them, mistaking a tendency for the whole personality. However, if someone is behaving in, say, an indecisive way, you should ask yourself what aspects of the negotiation may be contributing to this behaviour, rather than just saying to yourself, "Well, what do you expect – that's what they're always like." Never forget that, whether you are enjoying it or not, you are negotiating with this person because you each have something that the other wants. It is your duty to find ways to understand and, in so doing, to overcome their negative behaviour in order to reach a successful outcome.

Our tendency to label or judge is not limited to other people: we are equally capable of labelling ourselves. Try Work Solution 14, opposite, to explore some of the labels that we give ourselves and others, or think that others may attach to us, and consider ways to alter our negative perceptions.

WORK SOLUTION 14

Put a positive spin on negative behaviour

The way in which we perceive and are perceived by others can have a positive or negative effect on the climate of our negotiations. Therefore, it is important that we increase our awareness of the various images that we project and form. In this exercise we focus on the characteristics or labels that we apply to ourselves and other people and consider positive ways to transform them.

1. Make a list of three or four words that you would use to describe yourself (for example: "impulsive, friendly, understanding"). Then make another list of three or four words that describe the way that you think your colleagues see you. Compare the two lists – what do you see? The lists may be the same, but it is more likely that you will see some contradictions.

2. Next choose somebody you know from your working life with whom you have a difficult relationship. What labels do you attach to them? Again write a three- to four-word list. Now imagine how they might see themselves. If that is too difficult, look at the list you have just made and next to any negative qualities write a positive alternative (for example, "over-critical, impatient, arrogant" could become "exacting, dynamic, self-confident").

3. Think back to incidents that have influenced your negative perception of the person. Replay the episodes with the list of positive attributes you came up with in step 2 at the front of your mind. Try to see the incident through the eyes of the other person. How might *they* have viewed *your* conduct? Search your memory for any extenuating circumstances that might explain their behaviour.

4. Next time you deal with this person, do so in the positive frame of mind that you have engendered through this exercise.

THE "I WIN, YOU LOSE" NEGOTIATOR

From time to time you will have to deal with people who strongly believe that in any negotiation there is a winner and a loser. Of course, they will go to great lengths to ensure that they come out on top at your expense. As far as they're concerned, compromises are for other people. They are convinced that they are right and you are wrong. They may be demanding, confrontational, or even threatening. There are many possible reasons for this behaviour. Perhaps being on the attack is the only negotiating technique they know; perhaps they fear being seen to give in or back down; perhaps they feel their job is on the line. As with all negotiations, it is essential to focus on the true purpose of the negotiation and to concentrate on maintaining a good, positive climate. Your particular challenge when faced with an "I win, you lose" negotiator is to shift the climate from one of competition to one of cooperation – to show him or her that you can both win.

The "I win, you lose" negotiator is following a completely different set of rules from you. If you tried to persuade them directly of the benefits of an "everybody wins" philosophy, they would more than likely look at you in incomprehension. What is required is a more subtle approach – you need to give the impression that you are playing their game, while never losing sight of your principles.

For example, if the other party is not prepared to agree to anything that isn't their idea, then cultivate the technique of presenting your point as if it builds on their argument rather than knocks it down. If you do have to counter one of their proposals, package everything you say in terms of their needs, keeping your own firmly in the background. For example, if they make a demand that threatens your needs, explain to them how fulfilling their requirement could cause them to lose out. Suppose that they want to cut costs on a product you are manufacturing for them by using inferior materials. You might point out that this move risks damaging their credibility in the marketplace. Don't reveal your fears that it will undermine your company's reputation.

Avoid trying to break through resistance – an "I win, you lose" negotiator is dogmatic by nature and their stubbornness will only worsen if they feel they are being pushed. If they are confrontational, threatening or demanding, do not rise to the provocation or be cowed by the intimidation. Your automatic response may be one of anger or frustration, but by forbearing (see p.56) you neutralize their behaviour. Slow down your breathing (see p.97) to control your reaction – stay focused on the point of negotiation under discussion. In this way you will confound them by doing the opposite of what they expect. If they are on the attack they will expect you to be too: instead, think of them not as an enemy, but as a friend to whom you are offering support. Take their side, find ways to agree with them. Rather than replying to them with "But …", rephrase your response, by saying "Yes, I see your point, and … ." By doing this you are making it easier for them to say yes too.

THE BULLY

Bullying manifests itself in such a wide variety of behaviours that it can be difficult to recognize. At the crude end of the scale is the classic image of the bully in action: an overly aggressive individual browbeating his or her opponent into submission by shouting, threatening or blackmailing. However, bullying can be far more subtle than that. Mocking someone, ostracizing them or undermining their status or confidence are all examples of bullying behaviour.

On one level, the bully may wish to demonstrate his or her superiority to you – in terms of status, competence or experience. Perhaps their need for esteem has been threatened by their being assigned to a negotiation that they feel is beneath them. While annoying, this type of bullying is harmless. The best way of dealing with it is to indulge it. Show deference to the other party, make it clear to them how much you appreciate someone of their status becoming involved in this matter. Your task is to repair any damage to their self-esteem in order to make them an easier person to deal with.

However, where bullying takes on a more threatening aspect is in its aim to intimidate or infuriate you into a rash reaction. When you lose your cool, you lose sight of your objectives. Never let the bully do this to you. Use the Work Solution opposite to stay focused on the issues.

Above all, don't take bullying personally. It is merely a tactic that the other party uses time and again to get their own way.

WORK SOLUTION 15

Deflect the insult

In a negotiation, bullying may be deliberately employed as a technique to intimidate you and force you into a quick settlement. Regardless of whether the bullying behaviour is strategic or automatic, your negotiating challenge is to learn ways to stand up to the bully. Remind yourself not to take any of his or her comments to heart, even if they are apparently made as direct personal attacks. When confronted with a cutting remark, ignore it and stay focused on the aspect of negotiation under discussion. If you feel tempted to make a sarcastic rejoinder, say nothing. Simply stop and refocus yourself by following the steps below.

1. Take deep breaths and try to relax, imagining that as you exhale you are getting rid of any tension or negative emotion that you are holding in your body.

2. Adjust your position so that you are sitting or standing comfortably. Make sure both feet are placed firmly on the floor and (if standing) that your weight is evenly distributed between them. This will help you to feel grounded again if you have been "knocked off balance" by the bully's tactics.

3. Turn your focus back to the bully – visualize him or her as a small child having a tantrum, or as a badly behaved puppy, or imagine them slowly shrinking until they are a few inches tall and can only make a barely audible squeak.

4. When you are ready to speak, make no reference to the bully's behaviour. Adopt good eye contact. Make a conscious effort to speak slowly, calmly and clearly. Try to bring everyone's attention back to the negotiation process. For example, if the other party is unhappy with the service that your company is providing, seek ways to remedy the problem.

THE LIAR

We all exaggerate or bend the truth from time to time, but in negotiation someone who is lying can be a particularly tricky opponent. Lying is possibly the most complex of all the negotiation characteristics you might encounter. Someone who lies is a "trickster" and can manifest positive and negative personality traits (he or she can be charming or manipulative). The person's effectiveness as a liar depends upon whether or not we are convinced by his or her sincerity; while our challenge is to recognize the signs and prevent the lying from undermining the process of fair negotiation. Work Solution 16 on the opposite page will help you to meet this challenge and keep the negotiation climate safe.

There are no certainties in dealing with liars. All you can do is make sure that your preparation is as thorough as possible so that you are fully aware of the facts and figures relevant to the negotiation. Keep notes on any details or agreements made between you, and offer to supply the other party with a copy of your notes. Double-check all facts before coming to a final agreement. Never be afraid to refer to your notes, or to suggest a break in which to verify a piece of information. Bear in mind that factual inconsistencies alone do not necessarily prove that an individual is lying.

However, if you are sure that you are being misled, you should confront the other party and ask him or her to explain any inconsistencies. Even if they react with indignation and are reluctant to give you a response, they will realize that you have recognized their tactics and that you are not afraid of confronting him or her about them.

WORK SOLUTION 16

The lie detector

A skilled liar will rarely betray him- or herself by word or gesture alone. Use your intuition – if something doesn't feel right, it probably isn't. Then, try the following steps to identify signs that support your hunch. One sign alone might not be conclusive; but two or more could provide clear indication that the information the other party is giving you should not be taken at face value.

1. Be alert to contradictions, inconsistencies or ambiguities in information the negotiator presents as fact (details such as completion dates or unit costs). Does the other party offer information as fact and then later retract or alter it?

2. Look out for meta-talk (see pp.76–8). Treat sceptically information that is accompanied by phrases such as "Trust me", "To tell the truth", "Frankly ...", "Honestly ..." or "I would never lie to you."

3. Be aware of nonverbal signs of lying. Some common indicators are: difficulty in making eye contact, coughing, throat-clearing, touching the nose or pulling on an ear lobe when speaking, or sweating visibly even in a cool room.

4. Does the negotiator behave evasively? Does he or she attempt to sidetrack your questions, distract you, or embarrass you for trying to protect your own interests (for example, when you ask to check facts with colleagues or experts)?

5. Once you are certain that you are being lied to, take steps to confront the other party. Remain calm, always protecting the climate, and gently but firmly point out any inconsistencies you have noticed and insist upon clarification. Ask for written confirmation of everything that you have discussed and agreed upon.

THE INDECISIVE DECISION-MAKER

The indecisive decision-maker may be easier to negotiate with than the person who states, "Once I make up my mind, I never change it", but his or her inability to make a decision may prove frustrating and bring out the worst in you.

Let's take a look at this first. The indecisive person is not necessarily aware of the effect his or her actions have on you, although they might guess from your nonverbal behaviour that something is amiss. If you find yourself in this type of situation, the first thing to do is to clarify in your own mind why you find the behaviour so irritating. Consider also whether you might be contributing to their indecisiveness.

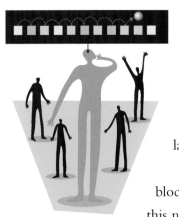

Mentally step back from the situation and observe. If you feel angry or annoyed, do not allow yourself to react.

Now that you are calm, you are ready to deal with the problem you face. Indecisiveness is usually the result of a fear of taking risks, lack of information, lack of trust, lack of authority, or perfectionism.

Once you can pinpoint the reason for the block and provide a remedy, you will probably find this negotiator more forthcoming and more willing to see new ways of looking at the negotiation than a person with a fixed point of view.

You will need to focus on keeping the negotiation moving forward. Avoid signalling to the other party that you have recognized their difficulty as this will exacerbate the problem. Take the role of mentor and find ways to help the other person develop confidence in their ability to make decisions. Bring up small points that can be resolved easily (even obviously), or point out areas where you are both in agreement. Acknowledge and show gratitude for the other party's ability to see all aspects of the negotiation – especially if this includes avenues that you had not considered. Ask if there is any information you can provide to help close the decision-making process. Pay attention to what needs you might be failing to address in the other person: are their esteem needs unfulfilled? How could you rectify this?

Make sure you are not trying to force a deal on someone who is not ready to negotiate – indecisiveness may be a signal that you are going too fast. Maybe they intended only a preliminary discussion and are not yet ready to negotiate all the points on offer. If this is the case, suggest an adjournment and schedule a new meeting at a later date – make it clear that the agenda for that meeting will be to resolve all the issues and strike a deal. If they are unable to agree to a date, find out why not – there may be sound reasons why they are stalling. Remember that there is little value in forcing an agreement – the other party will only regret their decision, and they may try to renegotiate soon after. At worst, they may feel bullied and not want to deal with you again.

There may be times when a negotiator doesn't have the authority to make a decision. Ask them directly whether this is the case. If it is, find out who does have the authority and adjourn the negotiation until that person can be consulted or is able to be present at the negotiation.

THE PERFECTIONIST

Perfectionism in business has both positive and negative aspects. A perfectionist will be fully prepared for a negotiation, ready to present you with the documentation you need to make the deal. He or she is reliable and will most often meet agreed deadlines and keep appointments. A perfectionist will thoroughly research the implications before making a deal. This means that you can totally rely upon any agreement you reach, even if it takes a while to get there.

On the down side, perfectionists tend to be control freaks (believing that no one else is capable of their high standards). They can become so fixated on details that they may lose sight of the bigger, more fundamental aspects of the negotiation. Perfectionism often leads to difficulty in being able to deviate from a considered strategy, which can make it difficult for the perfectionist to recognize, address, and adapt to your party's needs. The uncertainty of suddenly having to think of an alternative approach may be stressful for a perfectionist. The manner in which a perfectionist talks can be exacting, questioning or unconvinced.

However, perhaps worst of all, perfectionism often leads to procrastination. The act of making a decision can seem the ultimate test of a perfectionist's planning strategy. They may seem overcome by a fear that in the end the decision won't reflect their time and effort – the result won't be as perfect as the planning.

As the other party, you must try to do everything in

your power to keep the negotiation moving forward. If you know in advance that you will be negotiating with a perfectionist, ensure that you draw up a detailed agenda for the meeting and circulate it to all parties beforehand. Not only will this give you a map by which to travel your negotiation, it will also highlight the number of issues you have to get through in the time. Do make sure that you allocate time at the end of the agenda for dealing with specifics – there is no point in trying to dodge the fact that you will have to discuss detail. If the perfectionist starts to draw you into detail early in the negotiation, be appreciative of the points he or she raises, make notes to demonstrate that you are listening and then gently but firmly press on, making clear that you will come back to those points once the broader matters are settled. Never dismiss the detail – remember that often the most important information in a contract is in the small print and the details should be important to you, too. If the negotiation is at a standstill, introduce a brainstorming session to encourage creativity. Always be prepared to illustrate new ideas in a positive light and be able to back up alternatives with documents, facts and figures – this will save time.

When the time comes to close the deal, remember that a perfectionist will back off if they feel pressured. Allow some thinking time – break for lunch or a coffee, if you can. If the other party comes back with questions, keep your body language open and give straightforward answers. Once all the questions are answered, ask for commitment.

THE UNRESPONSIVE NEGOTIATOR

Attempting to negotiate with someone who just won't engage can be unnerving. If they refuse to take the initiative in conversation or to answer your questions in the detail that is required to move the negotiation forward it can also be exhausting. The danger is that your uneasiness may make you gabble to compensate for their unresponsiveness, perhaps even conceding objectives in the process.

Some people are shy, unforthcoming or distrustful by nature. With these people, it may take longer than usual to break the ice. The key is to create a climate of warmth and trust. Marilyn Kane, a prominent New York real-estate entrepreneur, does a routine check on people with whom she is negotiating to find out background information such as their interests and family details. People who are hard to communicate with are often impressed and may open up a little if you show interest in something significant about them beyond this particular deal. Try also giving them some information about yourself. Hopefully this will lower the barriers, perhaps even make you seem human and vulnerable, too.

One simple explanation for the other party's reticence may be that he or she is not a native speaker of the language in which the negotiation is being conducted. If this is the case, make sure that you are not going too fast for them. Summarize at intervals – for example: "You like the product but don't want to spend that much money. Is that correct?"

Harder to deal with is "poker-face" behaviour that is used as a deliberate tactic to unnerve you into revealing sensitive information or making a concession. Negotiators who say very little because they are shy or having to use a non-native language will still give information nonverbally. However, those who use unresponsiveness as a tactic will keep their gestures under as tight a rein as their words. This makes it difficult to gain any insight into their needs or objectives. You might consider pointing out gently to them that you are seeking an outcome that meets their needs (as well as yours), but that you will not be able to achieve this aim if you do not know what their needs are.

Whatever the reason for the other party's unforthcoming behaviour, there are moves you can make to overcome it.

It's pretty clear that you will have to take the lead in discussions. Although this may be taxing, it does give you the opportunity to set the agenda and the pace of the negotiation. Don't hand over control of the negotiating pace to the other party by gabbling – instead take advantage of the gaps they leave to consider your next moves.

Draw the other party out by asking questions requiring more than a "yes" or "no" answer and be precise about the information you require. "How was the meeting?" is not as effective as "What topics were discussed?" When they do speak, be very attentive and use their own words to elicit further information. For example, if they say, "There may be a problem with the supervisor", repeat the key words back to them: "Problem with the supervisor?" However, respect any information that they reveal to you: never use it to attack or undermine them.

THE FLATTERER

We have all succumbed to flattery at some time or another –
even at work. Only the most surefooted of us can say that we
haven't rounded our expectations downward or our commit-
ments upward because, say, the CEO has complimented a
presentation we just gave or a report we just submitted or a
particularly lucrative deal we just struck. Flattery is one of the
most obvious of all negotiation traps – and yet for many of
us one of the most irresistible. Why? The answer is simple:
flattery plays into the hands of our esteem needs. We feel
good when we think someone respects us or appreciates our
efforts. Physically, we get a "happy rush" – our body releases
hormones that make us feel more alert and positive. For

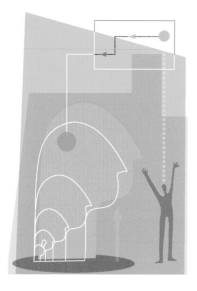

the other party, these reactions are perfect –
during our feel-good phase we let down
our guard and, unless we check ourselves, we
feel compelled to return the compliment.
However, in more cases than we care to men-
tion, returning the favour means revising
objectives downward and conceding where
we should hold firm.

So, time for a reality check. You are bril-
liant at what you do; you are a valued and
committed member of your team; you are
also a great negotiator, a successful business
person and you take a highly intelligent
approach to your work. None of these things means that
you do not deserve or warrant the objectives you have set
yourself in your negotiation.

There is really only one tactic to defend yourself against flattery – accept it, let it go and keep your focus firmly on your objectives. Reading the climate is an important tool here. If you know the other party well, and you know that you can use humour to defuse the situation, make light of the flatterer's attempts. Keep your tone jovial, smile and say something like "Thank you, but that won't work – let's just stick to the issues!" If you feel that humour would be inappropriate, you can be more serious: "I'm delighted that you think that, but it's important that we focus on the issue here ... ." Or if the flattery is directly related to the way you have presented a specific point in the negotiation: "I'm delighted that you think that – this is a really important point for me and the right outcome could work well for both of us", and return straight to the matter in hand.

Be aware that flattery is sometimes used to get you to lower your expectations because the other party hasn't prepared as well as he or she should have. By flattering you they hope to be able to mask their lack of knowledge – hoping that you will concede more easily without pursuing specific issues or asking them "difficult" questions. Flattery may also be an ill-judged effort to establish a good rapport with you, or a genuine (if inappropriate) expression of admiration for you. Whatever the reasons, always be wary of it – hold firm, remind yourself of your objectives, accept the flattery and move on swiftly. Soon enough the flatterer will become bored with their attempts to distract you, and the appropriate negotiating climate will be restored.

YOU AS THE DIFFICULT PERSON

When relations with the other party chill, do not discount the possibility that you are the person who is causing the problem. If you are lacking in self-awareness, or have not previously had the opportunity to learn about how one individual can influence group dynamics, you may not realize that it is your behaviour that is hindering the negotiation.

To discover whether you're the one who is being difficult, watch people's reactions to comments or gestures that you make. You can infer their disapproval from their nonverbal signals. For example, if they sigh, it may indicate that you are labouring your point, while squirming in their seats may be a sign that you are overloading them with information or tak-

ing an approach that makes them uncomfortable or agitated. Visibly mounting anger may be a response to your obstructiveness. If they whisper to each other, they may be sharing their disapproval at something you have said or done.

What annoys you in other people? Do the traits that you hate to see in others feature in your own behaviour? If you perceive that you are causing offence but you cannot see why, bring in a trusted associate to observe you, help determine what the problem might be and suggest positive ways to adjust your behaviour.

There could even be invisible causes. Maybe you replaced someone who was loved and is missed – you are difficult, not through any fault of your own, but because your presence represents your esteemed predecessor's absence.

WORK SOLUTION 17

See yourself as others see you

The key to seeing yourself as others see you lies in your self-awareness and your awareness of any feedback that other people give you. This exercise is designed to heighten your sensitivity to signs that your behaviour may be causing offence or disapproval. Once you have identified your "difficult triggers" you can modify that behaviour, to help restore a climate in which you can all seek creative solutions. Are you prepared to apologize for the way you've behaved in the past? Could you make a commitment to correcting your behaviour in the future?

1. Look out for patterns in your behaviour that might obviously create negotiation difficulties. For example, do you interrupt to get your view across? Do you have a tendency to be long-winded? Do you become angry quickly?

2. Look back through the topics covered in this chapter. Do any of them apply to you. For example, are you a perfectionist? Are you fearful of making concessions even when you will gain as a result?

3. Ask your friends and family (and your colleagues if you know them well), in the spirit of lightheartedness, to tell you what makes you difficult to deal with. They may say you are stubborn, pushy or indecisive – or many other things. Consider how these behaviours might affect a negotiating climate. Find ways to channel your negative traits in a positive direction. For example, transform pushiness into assertiveness by clearing space for a less assertive negotiator to speak rather than talking over him or her yourself.

4. Pay attention to the nonverbal feedback you receive during a negotiation. Take a pause to think about these reactions and assess what caused them. Refocus your attention onto your objective of seeing this negotiation to a satisfactory conclusion.

chapter 5

SETTINGS AND SITUATIONS

In the previous chapter we examined how to modify our negotiating style to accommodate various types of difficult behaviours. In this chapter we will see that we have to adapt not only to the particular characteristics of the people with whom we negotiate but also to the context of the negotiation. Specific situations such as a job interview, a performance review or an act of delegation each require a distinct strategy. In each case there are certain types of research to conduct, questions to ask and pitfalls to avoid. Similarly, our approach will differ depending on whether we are negotiating as an individual entrepreneur or in a team, from a position of strength or a position of weakness, whether we are dealing face to face, over the phone or by e-mail.

However, never forget that in all negotiations an "everybody wins" philosophy and the elements of the Foundation should lie at the heart of our strategy. By adhering to these principles, we stand the best chance of reaching a successful outcome whatever the situation.

TELE-NEGOTIATION

Much of the language of negotiation presumes a face-to-face interaction. We talk about putting an offer on the table, shaking hands on a deal, seeing eye to eye. However, geographical constraints and tight schedules mean that many negotiations are conducted between people who never meet. These long-distance negotiations present different challenges from face-to-face dealings. In this section, we will look at how we can overcome the limitations and exploit the advantages of the two most common tele-negotiation channels: telephone and e-mail.

In a face-to-face negotiation we can make use of the full range of nonverbal cues (see pp.72–5), in order to convey our message and influence the negotiating climate, and to discern

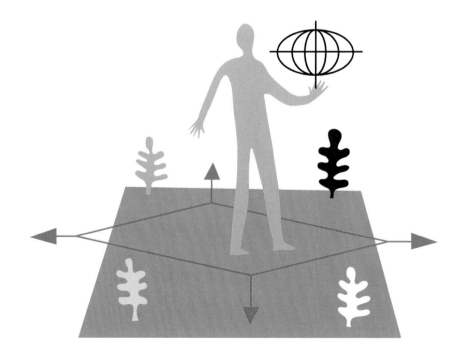

the mood, concerns and motivations of the other party. And there is usually some scope to build close, cooperative relationships: for example, by chatting informally during coffee or lunch breaks.

Many of these benefits are unavailable to us when the other party is at the end of a phone line rather than across a table. However, although it may seem less of an event in your working day, a phone call often constitutes just as vital a stage in your negotiation as a face-to-face meeting. Treat a call with respect. The chances are that you will know the call is coming, so prepare in advance systematically by analyzing and noting down your needs and objectives. Ask yourself how you want the negotiation to develop as a result of this call – ideally, write out an agenda. Pay particular attention to the opening section of the conversation, which is where you should explain to the other party what ground you want to cover. A strong, confident opening sets the tone for the rest of the call. Write down a list of questions (see pp.68–71), the answers to which will help you understand better the other party's needs. One distinct advantage of communicating by phone is that you can refer easily to your notes: exploit this advantage keeping them close at hand (ensure that they are clearly filed and labelled beforehand).

For the very reason that preparing for a phone negotiation is so crucial, be wary of springing an important call on the other party without warning, pressing them to react immediately to your questions or proposals. You may be tempted to take the upper hand in this way, but such an

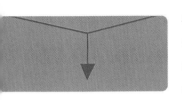

approach is almost guaranteed to damage the climate. The other party's trust in you will be badly shaken, making a successful outcome harder to achieve. Instead, arrange an appointment for your next call, either at the end of your previous conversation or in an e-mail.

When negotiating by phone, we are not entirely bereft of nonverbal signals. Listen carefully for clues in the tone of voice of the person to whom you are speaking and act on them. For example, hesitation, stammering or throat-clearing may indicate that the other party feels uncertain – perhaps you should summarize the main points of the discussion and make sure they are happy with them.

In contrast, e-mail is a purely verbal medium. Because the words in an e-mail form the entirety of your message, take great care when choosing them (see Work Solution 18, opposite). Be particularly cautious with humour. Without the appropriate tone of voice or facial expression to signal that a comment is meant as a joke, it could be misinterpreted in a way that the recipient finds insulting or confusing.

Above all, remember that e-mail is not suitable for all phases of a negotiation. It is undoubtedly easier to write an e-mail telling a supplier that your company wants to cancel a contract than it would be to tell them over the phone or in person. You may wish to avoid a confrontation, but the damage you may do to the climate by using e-mail inappropriately may ultimately make a confrontation more likely. Before you start typing, ask yourself how you would react to this information popping up on your monitor. Would you prefer to receive the news via a conversation?

WORK SOLUTION 18

Take a cyber-pause

Many people find it harder to read and write accurately on screen than on paper. It is all too easy to skim over and miss an important detail when you are reading or writing an e-mail. Fortunately, e-mail is a medium that lends itself well to a pause for reflection. Before you click on "send", run your message through the following series of checks to ensure that your communication moves the negotiation forward.

1. If you are responding to an e-mail from the other party, re-read their initial message. Does your reply answer all their questions in a clearly signposted way? If you do not understand some of their questions, does your message ask for clarification – a better policy than ignoring them.

2. Next, focus on what you are requesting from the other party. Will it be clear to them what questions you want them to answer or what actions you want them to take? Consider including a list of action points at the end of the message.

3. Now it's time for a humour sweep. Re-read your e-mail, looking out for any jokes or wry, flippant or sarcastic comments. Make an effort to read any such comments through the eyes of the person who will be receiving the message. Is there a risk that they might either not pick up on the joke or, worse, take offence?

4. Do you sense, from your correspondence with the other party, that they value accurate grammar and spelling? If so, print out the e-mail and proofread it thoroughly. If it constitutes a particularly crucial stage in the negotiation, consider asking one of your colleagues to cast a second pair of eyes over it.

5. Make any necessary amendments, then – and only then – click on "send".

THE JOB INTERVIEW

When you attend a job interview with a potential employer it is important to remember that the interview is a negotiation – a two-way discussion in which both parties have needs that should be respected and from which both stand to gain something if an agreement is reached. Approach the interview as you would any other negotiation: keep the five elements of the Foundation in mind, and don't forget that if you feel confident you will come across well.

As with all negotiations, preparation is crucial, so make sure that you do your homework thoroughly before the interview (see Work Solution 19, opposite). During the interview, ensure that you make your needs clear, and ask questions if you require more information on the employer's needs. Demonstrate that you understand his or her need to hire the person who best fulfils the requirements of the job, and try to tailor all your responses to show how you fit the bill.

The final stage of a job interview usually involves negotiating salary and conditions. Show that you are prepared to make concessions, as long as they are reciprocated. For example, if share options are not available, you could request an increase in your pension rights instead. Avoid accepting any package the interviewer offers because you are desperate for the job. By defending your position, within reason, you will make a much better impression. The interviewer will be aware that, if you do get the job, your strong negotiating skills will be of benefit to his or her company.

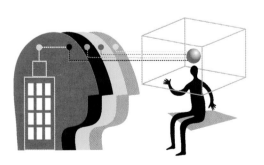

WORK SOLUTION 19

Do your homework

Interviews are negotiations that you need to prepare for zealously if you want to make the best possible impression. Give yourself plenty of time for a pause for reflection before the interview and use this time to take the following steps.

1. Gather information about your potential employer through library and internet sources, newspaper and magazine articles or contacts who work in the same field. Devise a short list of relevant questions about the firm that show that you have done your research and are genuinely interested in the company and its future.

2. Prepare answers for every question that you think the interviewer might ask. Rehearse speaking your answers onto a tape recorder and keep practising until you sound confident and poised.

3. Study the job description and think about the employer's needs. Be prepared to summarize any potentially useful areas of your experience, for example, "My web-design skills would be very helpful for your firm's new online service." If the post has requirements that you do not fulfil, think of positive ways of countering this, perhaps by pointing out other skills you have that are transferable, or by giving examples of occasions in the past when you have acquired a new skill quickly.

4. Write out a list of your own needs and objectives, in terms of salary and conditions, the skills you wish to put to use and the experience you hope to gain. Decide what kind of employment package you'll ask for and the least you're prepared to accept: list salary, vacation, pension and share-option requirements. Think about your priorities – for example, would you be prepared to accept a lower salary than the one you have now in exchange for longer paid vacation time?

NEGOTIATING YOUR WAY
UP THE LADDER

Nowadays promotions and raises are no longer awarded as a matter of course. In order to get a promotion you may be required to compete with outside applicants, while if you decide you want a salary increase, you may have to request it yourself and give justification for it even to be considered.

In the case of a promotion, make clear to your employer the reasons why you feel you should be promoted. Rather than outlining your needs, emphasize your accomplishments ("Since I came to this department, there has been a significant increase in profits") and your potential ("I have the ability and I'm ready for new challenges"). Give him or her a fact-filled summary of some of your most important qualifications ("I've demonstrated proven selling skills. I am capable of handling several projects at one time"). Your employer is more likely to consider you for promotion if they can see that your skills are currently being under-exploited.

Whether asking for a promotion or a raise, check beforehand that the salary you want is acceptable (see Work Solution 20, opposite), but allow your employer to suggest actual figures first. Be especially mindful of the climate – avoid aggressive moves, such as threatening to leave if you do not get what you are asking for (see pp.16–17). Such tactics are likely to create resentment and could result in your employer calling your bluff.

WORK SOLUTION 20

Understand your needs, know your value

Preparation is the key to success when asking for a raise or promotion. Understanding your needs and those of your employer allows you to plan exactly what to ask for. Knowing your own worth enables you to feel confident about requesting change. Before the negotiation, run through the following tasks.

1. Know your own needs and objectives. Ask yourself why you want this raise or promotion? Is it to increase your prestige, to improve your standard of living, to reassure yourself that your employer wants you to stay or to give yourself a new challenge? If your motivation is to improve your standard of living (security needs), you will focus on the financial aspect of a raise or promotion. If your reason is based on your esteem needs, or your desire for a challenge or change of direction, then the type of promotion will probably be more important to you than the salary.

2. Know your employer's needs. Has business been thriving recently or not? Is this a good time to request a raise or suggest a promotion?

3. Know your value. Research what the years of service in your job are worth in the general marketplace. Consult newspapers for job adverts, contact employment agencies, check salary statistics and, if possible, talk to colleagues who hold similar positions to yours.

4. Prepare to demonstrate your value to your employer by drawing up a list of tasks you have executed successfully in your current post. Also make a note of all the occasions on which you have performed above and beyond your job description. If you are requesting a promotion, list the ways in which you could contribute more to the company if you had a more senior position.

HIRING AND FIRING

Job interviews and the negotiation of employment or severance packages can be difficult situations for the manager con-
ducting them as well as for the candidate or staff member. If
these negotiations are not handled with great care both parties may suffer from more stress than is necessary, neither will
obtain all the information they need, and it could become
impossible to reach a satisfactory agreement.

Your challenge is to encourage an open exchange, and to
create and maintain as tension-free a climate as possible. An
informal setting can help to put both you and the other party
at ease: an office with a round table is a good choice.

Here are some pointers for an interviewer:

- *Before the interview, write out a list of simple, direct questions that
  will allow you to assess the candidate's suitability for the post.*
- *Give the interviewee your undivided attention and give verbal and
  nonverbal feedback to show your interest.*
- *Consider how the applicant will fit in with the other workers.*
- *Ask him or her how they would solve a specific problem. For
  example, if the post is managerial, "How would you handle an
  employee who complains about fellow workers?"*
- *Ask the interviewee to describe his or her biggest business failure.
  Assess how comfortable they are in showing weakness.*
- *Ask them where they hope to be professionally in five years' time.*

If you wish to take notes (in which case, do so unobtru-
sively) or record the interview, make sure the candidate is
comfortable with that. If you can, finish your questions

before giving a job description: this prevents the interviewee feeling pressurized to fit their answers to your requirements.

At the final stage, bring in details of the entire employment package: salary, holiday entitlement, health insurance and so on. Ensure you have considered the needs and objectives of both parties before you begin negotiating the terms of this package. Encourage the prospective employee to give their reactions to your proposal. If their salary needs exceed your budget, you may be able to offer terms that might appeal more than the extra money, such as a four-day week, flexi-time, or other lifestyle-enhancing options.

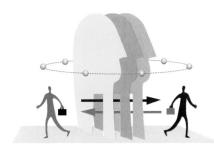

Firing an employee can be unpleasant for both parties, and the climate of the meeting is crucial if the dismissal is to be accomplished with as little pain as possible. Make sure you explain clearly why the employee is not meeting the company's needs, then allow him or her to put their point of view and listen attentively to what they have to say. It is vital that you recognize their need to salvage some self-esteem. Try to emphasize their strengths above their weaknesses – encourage them to think of it as an incompatibility problem rather than a personal rejection. Describe the company policy in terms of severance pay, outplacement help and any benefits and, if you can, make these terms negotiable; the more involved the employee is in the process the better. You could suggest a voluntary resignation – a face-saving device for them and a clean finish for you.

DELEGATING AUTHORITY

As an executive or manager, it is essential for you to delegate authority to ensure that work is done efficiently and on time. The delegation of a task should be negotiated with your staff – their input and their agreement will be crucial to the success of the project.

When negotiating the delegation of a job, first explain carefully the exact outcome you require and the deadline for completion – put this in writing where appropriate. Next, ask for feedback to make sure your requirements are clear and understood. Avoid giving prescriptive instructions as to how the employee should achieve the desired outcome in the allotted time. Instead, invite him or her to make suggestions as to how this can be accomplished – remember, staff often have additional experience and knowledge. By requesting and valuing their views you will encourage them to practise decision-making and make them feel more involved in the task.

Go on to define clearly the limits of delegated authority. For example, can the employee hire other people to work with him or her? Can they set their own budget for the project? You also need to ensure that the employee knows where he or she can obtain any further information that will be necessary for the completion of the job.

Finally, agree on a schedule for regular progress reports. If employees know in advance when to expect these discussions they can prepare for them and will feel encouraged by your continuing support.

HANDLING INTERNAL SQUABBLES

The employees who are most difficult to cope with tend to be those who regularly complain about their co-workers, and those who are always criticizing and blaming others. These people generate anger and resentment, and, as a result, internal squabbles often arise. When dealing with such issues, the manager's focus should be on creating and strengthening a positive climate in the workplace. Once you become aware of a problem between co-workers:

- *Negotiate with each party separately, listening without judgment or comment to what they have to say.*
- *If self-esteem or status is the underlying issue, assure each person of their value to the firm.*
- *If you need to make criticisms, address the issue at hand – never attack the individual.*
- *Give positive suggestions for correction and guidelines to avoid further confrontation – let the employees know that they can come to you should any subsequent problems emerge.*
- *Make it clear that you need your staff to work as a team, and that getting along with co-workers is therefore a prerequisite for keeping the job.*

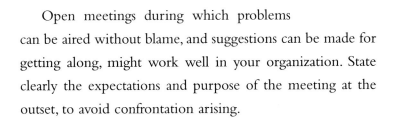

Open meetings during which problems can be aired without blame, and suggestions can be made for getting along, might work well in your organization. State clearly the expectations and purpose of the meeting at the outset, to avoid confrontation arising.

THE PERFORMANCE REVIEW

A performance review can lead to conflict between manager and employee. However, if handled sensitively it presents an invaluable opportunity for generating positive change.

Before chairing a performance review, take a pause for reflection to run through the elements of the Foundation.

needs and objectives

Think about your own needs and objectives and those of the employee. Remember, it is for you to find ways to improve the worker's performance. This is one of your objectives – one the employee probably shares. He or she also has esteem and fairness needs, while you need to obtain the best possible performance from him or her for the sake of the company.

facts

Make sure that you do your research thoroughly in advance. Employees need reliable evaluations: make sure that you have accurate information on each individual and the projects that they are involved in.

climate

A good climate is vital if both parties' needs and objectives are to be satisfied. As a manager, your task is to foster and maintain enthusiasm, and this meeting is an opportunity to do just that. Demonstrate to the employee that his or her input is valued, and seek to involve them in improving their own performance. Observe their verbal and nonverbal signs, especially if you need to criticize an aspect of their work. If

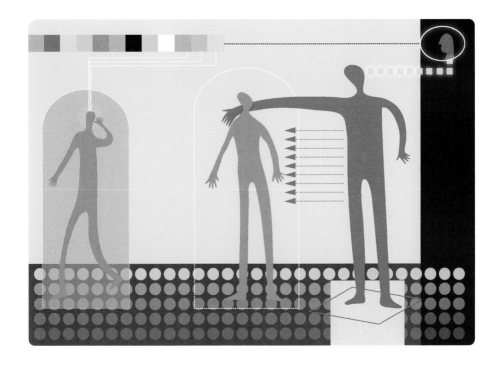

they shows signs of stress, try to rephrase your criticism to focus on the problem, not the person.

During the performance review:

• *Concentrate on an individual's current, not past, performance. This allows to you set realistic goals for the future.*

• *Encourage staff to suggest their own goals: "What do you want to accomplish in the coming year?" Invite them to suggest ways in which you can help them achieve those goals.*

• *When problems in performance arise, be specific: "You have missed three major deadlines in the last six months." Then make it clear to the employee that you will help to find a solution. Be constructive — consider ways to improve things in the future. Ask them what they think can be done to improve matters and how you can help.*

NEGOTIATING IN A TEAM

There are times where one-on-one negotiation is called for, but there are others when we need to work together as a team – many major industrial negotiations utilize large teams.

A team has the advantage of combining its members' abilities, and can benefit from more thorough advance planning and fact-finding than one person could manage. In addition, team members can look out for each other during a negotiation. For example, if one member starts to reveal too  much information, he or she can be given a pre-arranged signal to stop. However, team negotiations also have their pitfalls: the division of responsibility, if badly managed, can lead to chaos. A weaker member might be targeted by the other team, or, if the team members' roles are poorly defined, one person may speak out of turn. Thorough preparation is vital if we are to avoid these pitfalls.

In choosing your team, bear in mind that you are aiming for an effective, rather than an intimidating presence. Check how many people the other party will be sending and make sure that your team is of roughly the same size.

The first task during preparation is to set the team's goals. What concrete things will have to be accomplished during the negotiation in order for all the parties' needs and objectives to be satisfied? Draw up a plan detailing how your team can achieve this successful outcome.

The next stage is fact-finding. Divide up the background research between the various team members according to their areas of expertise, so that every area is covered.

Prior to the meeting, agree on the role that each person will play in the negotiation. It is a good idea to select a spokesperson to lead the proceedings. Team members with specific expertise (engineer, attorney, accountant and so on) usually only speak on matters pertaining to their area of knowledge at the request of the spokesperson. It is also useful to assign one or more team members to observe the gestures of the members of the other team. These observers can then report their conclusions at the next caucus, or even discreetly alert the team leader to any situation, such as a deterioration in climate, that needs to be dealt with straight away. You may also choose to elect a time-keeper and a note-taker. Agree that you will avoid changing roles during the actual negotiation, as this often causes confusion and can appear manipulative to the other team.

Once the roles have been attributed, discuss how your team will make decisions. Will this happen by consensus during breaks in the negotiation, or will the team leader have the final authority? If one person disagrees with the course the negotiation is taking should he or she request a pause so that the matter can be discussed by the team in private?

The final stage of preparing for a team negotiation is to have the team role-play possible scenarios based on a draft agenda. The aim is to allow the team to practise working together in a coordinated manner until each member feels comfortable with his or her role. Role-playing also allows any intra-team problems to surface and be dealt with before the negotiation itself.

BREAKING THE DEADLOCK

A deadlock occurs when both parties refuse to make further concessions to move the negotiation ahead. They have usually tried to explore alternatives (see pp.46–8), but have reached an impasse. Deadlock is always uncomfortable, and the possibility that the whole negotiation will founder can be extremely stressful.

The secret in dealing with a deadlock is to do everything you can to keep the negotiating process alive. If necessary, bring in additional people to help. You could even go to the other party's employer (see p.58) or employees – they may be able to offer alternatives you haven't considered.

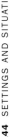

If none of these strategies works, and both sides recognize that the negotiation is in danger of collapsing, a mediator may be required. The mere presence of this third party can often effect a shift in the climate, inspiring people to come up with fresh possibilities for breaking the deadlock. A good mediator will seek to ensure that hostile attitudes are kept to a minimum and will try to lighten the mood. He or she will encourage each side to restate their positions and will explain each party's behaviour to the other so that any annoying attitudes can be seen in context and put into perspective. The mediator is often even able to suggest agreements on some issues that each side can accept without losing their bargaining position.

One example of mediation breaking a deadlock involved the case of a union member who had been fired for taking too many rest breaks. The union defended the man (even

WORK SOLUTION 21

Keep a foot in the door

When a negotiation is deadlocked both parties may decide to call a halt and stop negotiating while other, potentially drawn-out solutions, such as mediation or arbitration, are explored. At such times you need to use techniques to keep the lines of communication between the two parties open. Time changes everything and in a few days or weeks, people on both sides may have a change of heart – a resisting partner may have left or moved to a different department, or a mediator or arbitrator may call both parties back to the negotiating table.

Here are some steps you can take while you are waiting for the deadlock to be broken so that you can renew the negotiation process:

1. Keep in touch with the other party on a regular basis, and aim to keep your communication as friendly as possible. Try to begin each conversation with some personal small talk (ask questions such as "How are you?" or "Has your son recovered from his recent illness?"). Make it clear that you see the current deadlock as being over issues, rather than as a battle between individuals.

2. Show that you want to maintain openness by continuing to send any information that might be of interest to the other party. Inform them of any changes in the law or in your company's situation that relate to the issue you were negotiating, and encourage them to reciprocate by sharing any new information they might have with you. If you can, make a disclosure that may change the equation.

3. Be sensitive as to whether the other party is reacting adversely to your "keep-in-touch" phone calls. Perhaps an e-mail or fax might be easier for them to accept, especially if you need to communicate new information relating to the negotiation. However, just lengthen the interval between telephone calls, rather than stopping them entirely. A telephone conversation, however brief, forces the other party to respond to your efforts to keep the door to further progress open.

though the charges held up) because they thought that the management was simply trying to destroy the union. Management, on the other hand, refused to yield, as they presumed that the union was testing to see whether its members could ignore existing rules. A mediator was eventually brought in to reinterpret the actions to both sides. She succeeded in showing both the union and the management team that their views were misguided, the deadlock was broken and a satisfactory conclusion was reached.

In some extreme deadlock cases, arbitration may be called for – this is a drastic last resort. When they submit a dispute to arbitration, both parties are legally bound by the decision of the arbitrator. Many major negotiations (such as those between large companies and trade unions) are contractually bound to go into arbitration if a dispute cannot be satisfactorily concluded by the two parties alone. The main advantage of arbitration is that it can be an excellent opportunity for those involved to try hard to resolve the remaining troublesome issues by keeping the negotiation going even though they are in arbitration (see Work Solution 21, p.145). Indeed, arbitration often motivates the parties to come up with further alternatives in order to settle the disagreement before the arbitrator gives his or her ruling.

If, in spite of all your efforts, this negotiation is, indeed, doomed to fail, remember that you may find yourself negotiating with the same people at some point in the future. Continue to maintain a courteous relationship, for example through occasional telephone calls and e-mails, so that when the time comes you can present another deal to the party.

DEALING WITH EXPERTS

In cases where we need to consult an expert or bring one into the negotiation, or deal with an expert called in by the other party, we may find ourselves deferring to his or her expertise. However, we must remember that the expert is just another contributor, who, although able to provide specialist advice, is unlikely to have our vision of the bigger picture.

If you decide to call on an expert, arrange to meet with him or her at least once before the negotiation. Send a detailed agenda in advance, and provide a list of questions that you will need to ask them. At the end of your meeting, allow plenty of time for a brief summing up and questions to ensure that everyone has taken in the new information.

You may sometimes find yourself in a negotiation to which the other party has brought their own expert. Perhaps a client of yours has called on a technical expert to disparage your product in an attempt to get you to lower the price, or a company with whom you are involved in a difficult negotiation has brought a lawyer along. In such situations, it is important to avoid getting drawn into a technical discussion in which you are not qualified to participate. You need to bring the negotiation back onto a commercial footing as quickly as possible without damaging the climate. Listen attentively to the expert's points, ask precise questions about any key issues you do not understand, but do not try to counter his or her arguments. Instead, thank them for their input and request politely that they put their points in writing. Explain that you will then go over them with your own expert and give your responses at the next meeting.

NEGOTIATING
FROM A WEAK POSITION

Sometimes, particularly when we're negotiating with someone we feel in awe of, or if we're dealing with a matter that is very important to us, we feel that we're in a position of weakness. At these times it is important to remind ourselves of our own positive qualities, and of the reason for our presence at the negotiating table. The aim of any negotiation is to satisfy the needs of both parties – you clearly have something to offer the "stronger" party, otherwise he or she wouldn't be negotiating with you in the first place. Remember, the other party may not perceive your position as weak at all.

If you feel that you will be at a disadvantage in a negotiation, it can be especially beneficial to use the Foundation to help you with your preparations. Careful planning, and thinking about your strengths and what you have to offer the negotiation process will increase your self-confidence. If you can convince yourself of the positive aspects of your position you will also be able to convince others.

If the other party arrives at the negotiation believing that you are in a weak position, they may expect you to take a defensive stance. If you want them to listen to you, the best way to do this is to start by listening to them. Surprise them by agreeing with them as much as you can, but do not concede everything straight away – instead keep offering further alternatives. The other party may not have a clear picture of what they can gain from negotiating with you. It is up to you to help them to see how this deal can benefit both of you.

NEGOTIATING FROM A STRONG POSITION

Negotiating from a strong position offers us many opportunities. However, if we misuse this excess of power, we can place the whole negotiation in danger. For example, if such power is used to browbeat the other party it usually elicits anger, resentment and frustration, leading to the collapse of the talks. Another risk of abusing a strong position is that such behaviour may backfire at a later date – there is always a likelihood we will one day be dealing with the other party again, when they could be holding the power and may be tempted to retaliate.

However, a good negotiator can easily avoid these pitfalls. Being in a position of power provides you with a chance to put your positive negotiating skills into practice and to champion a conclusion in which both sides are winners. Also, if you have the luxury of knowing that you are in a strong position, you can focus your attention on maintaining a positive climate. Keep an eye on the other party's verbal and nonverbal signs – if you sense that they are feeling defensive, intimidated or anxious, reassure them that your aim is to truly understand their needs and to try to satisfy them as far as possible. Make it clear to them that you have an "everybody wins", not an "I win, you lose" approach.

Finally, bear in mind that the person you perceive to be on the weaker ground may, in fact, occupy a much more powerful position than you anticipated. Try not to make assumptions – if you do, be prepared to sometimes be surprised!

ADAPTING TO CULTURAL DIFFERENCES

Negotiators often need to deal with people from a different cultural background from their own. They may travel abroad for a meeting; they may play host to business partners from another country; or they may be negotiating with people who share their nationality, but are not from the same culture.

Cultural differences can affect every aspect of a negotiation, from time-keeping to tactics. Failure to take these differences into account can lead to the collapse of the negotiation.

In order to avoid misunderstandings and meet your objectives, you need to be aware of and sensitive to the culture of the party with whom you are negotiating. The key to this is thorough preparation. There are many ways of finding out about cultural differences before a negotiation: you could use libraries, newspapers, magazines and the Internet to glean

information, or talk to co-workers and friends who have experience of the culture concerned. You may even decide to use one of the many consulting firms specializing in this field.

When preparing for the negotiation, try to find out the answers to the following questions:

- *What are the social customs and behaviour of the other culture, including appropriate greetings, gift-giving and attitudes to time?*
- *Which gestures and other forms of nonverbal behaviour could be seen as offensive or rude by the other party?*
- *How much time should be spent socializing before beginning the negotiation? (In India, for example, talking about friends and family is an important part of establishing a business relationship.)*
- *How do attitudes to negotiating vary from those in your culture? (For Saudi Arabians, for example, saving face is very important, and you should be prepared to concede on an issue rather than risk humiliating a Saudi counterpart.)*
- *How might the other party's religious background affect the meeting? (For example, in many Islamic countries no business is done on Friday, the Muslim holy day.)*

If, during the negotiation, you sense that you may have inadvertently caused offence, or that a misunderstanding has arisen, move quickly to put things right. Do not be afraid to apologize and explain that you are not very familiar with the other party's culture, but that you are keen to learn about it.

NEGOTIATING
AS AN ENTREPRENEUR

Setting up and running your own business can be very rewarding. However, as an entrepreneur, you will face unique negotiating challenges, and the negotiations in which you engage during the early stages will be crucial to your success. You will probably find yourself negotiating with a bank manager first, as you seek financial backing. Later you will no doubt meet with potential customers and suppliers, all of whom may be used to dealing with larger companies.

When preparing for all of these negotiations, make use of the elements of the Foundation. Be clear on your objectives and analyze your needs. Do your research thoroughly. Always strive to sustain a positive climate in all your dealings.

When you approach a bank to apply for a start-up loan remember that this is a negotiation – both sides stand to win from a successful outcome. Think about the bank's needs and objectives (such as prompt repayments, long-term security) as

well as your own, and decide in advance how you can fulfil them. Present a clear business plan that outlines how you plan to finance your business, as well as detailing your proposed marketing plan, financial projections, pricing strategy, operating budget, loan-repayment schedule and so on. Ensure that you are as well-informed as possible about the details of any loan you may be taking on, and prepare a list of questions to take to the meeting to fill in any gaps in your knowledge. For

example, "If interest rates start to climb, can I lock in my loan before they rise higher?" or "What are my options if rates decline?" Do not be pressured into accepting the bank's first proposal – take time to consult a lawyer, accountant or broker, if necessary, and arrange another meeting for a later date.

Once your business is up and running, you will probably have to sell your product or service in competition with larger companies who can undercut your prices. You need to come up with other ways in which you can meet your customers' needs more effectively than your larger competitors. Maybe you are able to offer a unique personal service, which is at a premium in today's marketplace, while keeping your prices as reasonable as possible. Try to arrange face-to-face meetings with potential customers and demonstrate that you have thought about their needs and are able to fulfil them.

You may well also need to negotiate affordable prices with suppliers, even though your orders may be small compared to those of your competitors. Before meeting with suppliers, find out what they charge their large accounts so that you are not persuaded to pay a disproportionately high price. Plan ways of convincing the supplier that you will be a reliable customer. Use your first negotiation to begin building a good relationship with your suppliers. If they enjoy doing business with you they will be encouraged to give you a good rate to guarantee your continuing loyalty.

CONCLUSION

Now that you have worked through this book, embraced the principles and practised the skills, you should have had a chance to assess the effect that our ideas and suggestions have on your negotiations. The more often that you use the Foundation to prepare for, engage in and review your negotiations, the more natural the process will feel to you and the more successful you will be in meeting your objectives.

The beauty of an "everybody wins" philosophy combined with the elements of the Foundation is that they apply to all kinds of negotiation – from discussing bedtime with a five-year-old child to drawing up a trade agreement between two nations. No matter how high you rise in your career, you will not outgrow the principles on which this book is founded.

However, that is not to say that you will not continue to evolve as a negotiator. And there will always be room for improvement. Monitoring your progress will help you to ensure that you develop in a positive direction – correcting faults rather than introducing new ones. This is why it is such a good idea to review each of your negotiations and note key findings in a journal (see pp.43–5). Not only does it enable you to carry the lessons of your last negotiation into your next, but it also helps you to pick up and address any recurring long-term patterns in your performance that may be holding you back. For example, by analyzing the notes you have written over, say, the past year you might notice that in a significant proportion of cases your negotiations overran the allotted time, leading to costly delays in implementation. Armed with this insight you might consider focusing on ways to develop your time-management skills. Similarly, if you noted that different people in separate negotiations reacted to you in a particular, adverse way, you might look for something specific in your style that damages the climate. Without a permanent record to consult, you would not necessarily be aware that there was a pattern and so you would miss out on important opportunities for improvement.

Bear in mind also that looking out for trends in your negotiations does not only help you to identify faults to correct. There will be other occasions when you will be fortified by recognizing traits that contribute positively to a successful outcome.

At times you may find it wearing always to be the one who tries to keep the negotiation on track. Although your unilateral efforts to generate a cooperative climate and to seek a solution that benefits everyone will usually be recognized and, indeed, reciprocated by the other party, you will come up against negotiators who stick doggedly to an adversarial approach. In such cases you may be tempted to retaliate. However, once you lock horns it is very difficult to disentangle them. The most likely outcome is that neither party will gain anything, nor will they ever want to negotiate with the other again.

Never underestimate the significance of personal traits in business negotiations. Companies don't negotiate with each other – people do. Social skills *do* count. Honesty and reliability *do* count. An "everybody wins" philosophy *does* count.

Bramson, Robert M., *Coping with Difficult People*, Ballantine Books (New York), 1981

Fox, Jeffrey J., *How to Become a Rainmaker*, Hyperion (New York), 2000

Ilich, John, *The Art and Skill of Successful Negotiation*, Prentice Hall (Englewood Cliffs, NJ), 1973

Ilich, John and Barbara Schindler Jones, *Successful Negotiating Skills for Women*, Addison Wesley (Reading, MA), 1980

Korzybski, Alfred, *Manhood of Humanity* (second edition), The International Non-Aristotelian Library (Lakeville, CT), 1950

Korzybski, Alfred, *Science and Sanity* (fourth edition), The International Non-Aristotelian Library (Lakeville, CT), 1958

Kotter, John P., *The Heart of Change*, Harvard Business School (Cambridge, MA), 2002

Krass, Peter, ed., *Little Book of Business Wisdom*, John Wiley (New York), 2000

Maslow, Abraham, *Motivation and Personality*, Harper and Row (New York), 1954

Nierenberg, Gerard I., *The Complete Negotiator*, Barnes and Noble Books (New York), 1996

Nierenberg, Gerard I., *Negotiating the Big Sale*, Berkley Books (Mississauga, Ontario), 1992

Nierenberg, Gerard I. and Henry Calero, *How to Read a Person Like a Book*, Barnes and Noble Books (New York), 1996

Nierenberg, Gerard I. and Henry Calero, *Meta-Talk*, Cornerstone (New York), 1978

Nierenberg, Juliet and Irene S. Ross, *Women and the Art of Negotiating*, Barnes and Noble Books (New York), 1997

Nirenberg, Jesse, *Getting Through to People*, Prentice Hall (Englewood Cliffs, NJ), 1965

Pruitt, Dean G., *Negotiation Behavior*, Academic Press (New York), 1981

Scott, Bill, *The Skills of Negotiating*, Gower (Aldershot, England), 1982

Shapiro, Ronald M. and Mark Jankowski, *The Power of Nice*, John Wiley (New York), 1998

Smith, Manuel J., Ph.D., *When I Say No, I Feel Guilty*, Bantam Books (New York), 1975

Sparks, Donald B., *The Dynamics of Effective Negotiation*, Gulf (Houston, TX), 1993

Tavris, Carol, *Anger: The Misunderstood Emotion*, Simon and Schuster (New York), 1983

Weinberg, Harry L., *Levels of Knowing and Existence*, Hodder and Stoughton (London), 1960

Winston, Sandra, *The Entrepreneurial Woman*, Bantam Books (New York), 1979

INDEX

ACKNOWLEDGMENTS

We want to thank our editors at Duncan Baird Publishers for their excellent editorial help.